Prison Stories From Gladiator School

Robert Thorson

PublishAmerica
Baltimore

© 2011 by Robert Thorson.
All rights reserved. No part of this book may be reproduced, stored in a retrieval system or transmitted in any form or by any means without the prior written permission of the publishers, except by a reviewer who may quote brief passages in a review to be printed in a newspaper, magazine or journal.

First printing

PublishAmerica has allowed this work to remain exactly as the author intended, verbatim, without editorial input.

Softcover 978-1-4626-3482-8
PUBLISHED BY PUBLISHAMERICA, LLLP
www.publishamerica.com
Baltimore

Printed in the United States of America

Chapter One

It all started in the fall I was 17, I was stealing cars and just having a little illegal fun. I wasn't stripping the cars or anything, I was just joy riding.

Then, it just got to be too much of a good thing to keep to myself. So, I taught a few of *my good time friends* in the neighborhood how to steal cars too. Pretty soon there are four of us out there stealing cars and racing them on back roads. A couple cars did get wrecked. But most of them were just abandoned when they ran out of gas or when morning came.

On the morning of September 18, 1976, a group of Bikers that lived just down the street, showed up on my front porch. Yep, they were looking for you know who. So, being the tough guy I thought I was, with my hunting knife on my side, I went out to see what they wanted. Hell, there were only five of them, and I was fresh from Army Basic Training, 6 foot tall, 180 pounds and as dumb as a headless chicken and healthy as an ox.

It seemed that someone had stolen their 1960 black Ford Galaxy 500 Hot Rod and in the process of hotrodding around town, had blown up their brand new 390-cid engine. The engine probably just spun a bearing or something. But they weren't very amused by it and were looking to take it out on somebody or heck just about anybody would probably do.

They had it from a reliable source, my pal Lee, (the one who had actually stolen their car, and who was only like 5 foot 7 inches tall and 135 pounds) that it was me who had wrecked their Hotrod! Well of course they wanted me to pay for it, in one way or another. In fact, I'm thinking, they had it in mind to stomp a mud hole in my ass and walk it dry, whether I had the money to pay for the car or not, which as a matter of fact I didn't, so that was a moot point to began with.

About the time things started to get loud and ugly looking, my Momma came out of the house with a double-barreled 12 gauge shotgun. There she stood. All 5'7", 130 pounds of her, looking as proud as any Indian Princess with her long straight black hair, holding a shotgun at her shoulder sighting down the barrels like she knew what to do with it and there they all were, clustered up looking like a turkey shoot, no place to run or hide, if she pulled the trigger everyone was going to get some lead pellets. You would rather tackle on a grizzly bear then mess with my Momma when she was protecting one of her kids. Hell, she took a shotgun to school in my third year because a teacher had swatted me on the butt with a wooden paddle. She was raised hunting and shooting in Sioux Lookout, Ontario Canada.

So, when she suggested they mosey on and "Get the hell off my front porch!" as she so elegantly put it, they had the good sense not to argue with her while they were looking down the business end of a loaded 12 gauge double barreled shotgun.

Well, as you might guess, I had some explaining to do and got my tail about chewed off with the hollow warning that maybe next time she might just let the bikers have their way with me. But, such is the life of a young outlaw.

Later that night, about 6 O'clock, I was walking home from the store and I saw a biker. I don't know if it was one of them or not, as they all look about the same to me, but this one calls to me, "Robert, come here!" from across the street.

I pulled my knife and holding it behind my leg (in a handy position to use in a hurry, if need be), I say, "Whatchoo want?" in my best tough guy accent. About that time I notice he isn't alone, there is a second biker in the trees along the side of the road. I start walking towards home, being a tough guy I can't run, right? As I look back, I see that the first biker I encountered was pulling a gun from the inside of his black leather vest. I toss courage to the wind and beat feet like the Army taught me to. At a fast sprint, I leave them dorks in the dust. I run inside the house and into my bedroom where the guns are all stored and snatch up the shotgun.

My Momma comes in about then and says, "What's up?"

I tell her, "Them bikers are back, only this time they have guns."

She says, "Ok" and gets out of my line of fire. As we step into the front room.

About that time the front door flies open and in come the two bikers. I have them dead to rights and under the gun. My sister, Betty Jean, and my cousin, Steven, jump to the door to stop the intruders from coming into the house, but right in my line of fire. The bikers both have guns out but pointed in the wrong direction, so Betty yells, "Whatchoo want?" and Steven is yelling at them "Get the hell out of the house!"

The bikers then shout, "Police", so I put my gun down and my family clears their line of fire. They both swing their guns to target me. I see this might be the end, so I step backwards into my bedroom and slam the thick oak door shut. While standing there, I hear my sister scream, "You're going to kill my Mom!"

Then I hear a gun go off in the front room. But in my head I was so stressed I actually thought I had dropped the shotgun for a moment until I remembered it was in the front room. So I grab the Marlin 30/30 and start jacking' rounds into the breach, just then the door flies open and I have my back to the door and start to swing towards the opening door when I hear "Move one muscle and I will blow your fucken head off!" So I put the rifle down.

What happened in the front room was my Momma picked up the shotgun by the barrel near the top, so the butt of the rifle is a few inches off the ground and said, "Is this what you want?"

Undercover Officer Brown in a panic shouts, "Drop the firearm!"

My Momma said, "He doesn't have it, I do".

Not understanding that the cop was talking to her, she starts walking towards him. Undercover Officer Brown then cocks his .357 magnum service revolver and repeats his demand that my Momma drop the firearm and shoves his gun towards her stomach. She strikes his hand away from her in a downward motion and that is when his gun goes off into the floor, flash burning her hand, the bullet going into the floor by her feet. Then she finally understands that the cop is talking to her. So she puts the gun down.

That is when the undercover cops kick my bedroom door in and notice me loading a second weapon, The Marlin 30.30.

I was arrested and charged with second-degree assault. They had to justify discharging their firearm. Nothing was ever mentioned about the auto theft. From this point on it was all about the Second Degree Assault with a deadly weapon on two undercover police officers.

Someone had to be charged with something, so I ended up being the scapegoat. I was taken to the King County Jail, charged and booked for second degree assault with a deadly weapon then I was striped and fogged with bug spray from head to toe. I was then given a pair of jail coveralls and assigned to a tank with older felons and not allowed to shower that night.

Three days later I went in front of a judge for an arraignment hearing and I was given a public pretender, someone upon which to hang my faith, hope and trust. (A Court appointed attorney).

PRISON STORIES FROM GLADIATOR SCHOOL

From September until January, they went through all the motions of giving me a fair trial, back then I still believed in truth, justice the American way and all of that other nonsense. I thought since I was innocent, there was no way I could be convicted of anything. (Now, I know Justice is spelled "Just-Ice" for the poor, which means just put them on ice. Justice for the rich on the other hand is spelt "Just-Us" and the law is applied a little differently towards the rich then it is towards the poor.)

After all, the cops were *undercover* and never identified themselves. They admitted to that on the witness stand. Also, I thought these cops were bikers, with good cause, since I had been threatened by bikers just that morning, and these cops were dressed like bikers. Both wearing blue jeans, Officer Brown had a black leather vest on and the other cop was wearing a Levi jacket with the sleeves cut off. No reasonable man would have thought these were cops under those circumstances.

Although I had to spend my 18th birthday and Christmas in jail, I knew it was all just a big misunderstanding and all's well that end's well, right? A little jail time was ok too. It would do wonders for my reputation with the girls, as a bad boy.

After all, I had been stealing cars and joy riding, so I wasn't totally opposed to an outlaw rep. nor was I completely innocent.

I went through the trial with John Law, My Public Pretender. It was I am sure, one of his first cases, fresh out of law school and joined the Public Defender's Office. I would have been better off with no lawyer, but I didn't know that at the time. He didn't call all my witnesses. Heck he didn't even call my key witnesses. He said we didn't need them. He just called my mom, my sister and my cousin, just my family members if you will. I didn't know it back then, but the District Attorney's Office and the Public Defender's Office worked hand in hand with each other. Often they traded convictions for plea bargains, for letting someone off on some minor thing to get a conviction on a more serious crime. Guilt or innocence has little to do with it. They are trying to build reputations and track records. By not calling my non-related Key Witnesses that saw the street confrontation, it just looked like my family was trying to help me out of a difficult situation by telling a different story then the cops and DA told.

John Law kept trying to get me to take a plea bargain. But being not guilty of what I was charged with, I couldn't understand why I should plead guilty to it. I thought I would show him, when I was found Not Guilty. I must have thought there was some magic that happened to save innocent people and fools from being found guilty. I just knew after a fair trial, I would be acquitted. How was I to know I had no chance of winning? That my Attorney was working with the DA.

Now I know that there is no such thing as a fair trial in America. It doesn't matter what color or race you are. If you're poor you're going to be convicted. If you have money, you get a better result at the end . But it still isn't a fair trial. I was sold down the river for being poor. That was a big surprise to me back then, that innocent people could be sent to prison for crimes they didn't commit to protect law enforcement reputations and build DA's portfolios'. These convictions also serve to stem the flow of law suits for misconduct and abuse of authority against the police force.

After I was convicted, the jury wrote a letter to the Judge that said if my gun had been unloaded they would have found me not guilty. That they felt the police officers should have identified themselves before pulling their guns. But, since there are no self defense laws in the State of Washington at that time, they felt they had to find me guilty.

Have you ever tried to protect yourself with an empty gun against armed felons? Me neither, and wasn't about to start right then. Yes they were police but I had no way of knowing that at the time.

I was sure now, that since the judge had sat through the whole trial and read the letter the jury had wrote, he knew what a miscarriage of justice had occurred and at sentencing he would give me a suspended sentence or credit for time served. He would have to correct it somehow, right? He couldn't let me, an innocent man, go to prison for a crime he knew I had not committed.

He sentenced me to ten years.

Chapter Two

I was, then, sent to Shelton Receiving Center on February 9, 1977, where I was inducted, inspected, injected, dehumanized and they cut my long hair after the first of many fist fights with the goon squad. They would learn to dread seeing me before I was released.

I had to see the shrink after that and of course he told me that he didn't see anything wrong with me except, that I had a problem with authority figures. Well, duh.

A few weeks went by and I did dumb aptitude and personality tests and we all told each other about our own special crimes and tried to act as cool and tough as we could, some guys just couldn't pull it off and became victims for the rest of us.

Then came the big day, I got to go in front of The Board of Prison Terms and Paroles. I went in there with high hopes, I figured as soon as they were told how I had been railroaded into Prison, and how I wasn't really guilty, they would give me an immediate Parole. Hope springs eternal, doesn't it? Hope is a changeling that often blooms into dark despair. But I had nothing left but hope, so I kept raising the little changeling and it kept blossoming for me.

The court set the maximum term and the Board of Prison Terms and Paroles set the minimum term. I go in the boardroom. There are two old women sitting in the room behind one of those long wooden tables. They must have been at least 30 years old. I give them my version of events, as I understood and remembered them, of the night that things went so terribly wrong for me.

They told me to leave the room and wait for their decision. I figured it was all just about over. I hear the bell and go back inside the room with all the pretty wood walls and furniture, feeling good, I sit down smiling.

The chair person says, "Mr. Thorson, we find you to be a serious threat to society. The seriousness of your crime, who your victims were and the fact that you don't take any responsibility for your actions, nor admit to the crime, is a serious factor in our decision to sentence you to the minimum term of ten years".

I was in a state of shock, but I controlled it pretty well. I just sat there for a second, gathering my composure and then I asked, "Do y'all mind if I say somethin?"

"No, go ahead Mr. Thorson," one of them replied.

So, I calmly said, "I think your both a couple of fucking whores!" then I stood up and grabbed what I thought was hot coffee in cups in front of the ladies and threw it into their faces. It turned out to be just cold water. But they needed the wakeup call anyway, so it wasn't a complete wasted effort. Man I was devastated, angry and disillusioned.

Then I walked out of the room and tried to leave and go back to my cell. But one of the ladies stuck her head out of the room and snitched me off!

She exclaimed, "He just threw water on us!" Her make-up was running down her face, it was great.

The guard, who was opening the door for me pulls it back closed and asked, "Did you do that?"

"Yep"

"What did you do that for?"

"Cuz I wanted to"

"Well, I hope in that case, you wanted to see our hole too" by the hole he meant the Segregation Unit.

I did a short stay in the hole but it wasn't too bad. Then by the time I got out all the new guys I was with in receiving had heard all about it. None of them had been to the hole, and I threw water on the Parole Board, so I was like the coolest of the new guys.

I had to go see the shrink again because of my behavior. This time he told me I was going to Washington State Reformatory at Monroe, also known as Gladiator School. That I was only going to make it there one of two ways, because my tough guy act wouldn't work there and that I would either have to pay for protection or be somebody's punk.

(A punk is a person turned in to a sex object by force. Not as much of that happens in the joint as Hollywood would have you believe, as there are a lot of homosexuals in the joint just looking for someone to give it up to. Anyone that wants to partake of that sort of thing doesn't have to look far or take it by force unless that is the way he likes it. But that never really interested me. I like girls and always will. Guys that go to prison and become lovers of men, were always lovers of men and were just waiting for the right time and place to let it show. A lot of guys say "Just because I let the boy suck my dick doesn't mean I am gay, or just because I fucked the boy in the butt don't make me gay. Well, I have to tell you, it doesn't matter what position you play, if you're in the game, you're on the team.)

Chapter Three

Well, I went to WSR (Washington Start Reformatory) at Monroe just as the shrink predicted. My first cell was on C-side also known as The Reservation, because mostly only Native Americans lived there. (We called them Indians back then.) Whoever had lived in my cell before me had written in big words, above the door, on the inside of the cell, "May it ever be so humble, There is no place like home." At that time I had no idea how long prison would truly be my home, nor how comfortable I would eventually get in there. I did get beat up and robbed a few times but I am too ugly to be considered a serious sex object, I look like a white Danny Glover. The fourth or fifth day I was there, I got a food and clothing package from home. The next day I was asked if I wanted to sell any of my clothes.

"No", I said.

So then I was asked if I would like to smoke a joint with this guy and a couple of his friends, naturally I agreed, because I had on a cool hat ,jacket and boots I figured they just naturally would want to hang out with me and be my friend. So I walked willing into a blind spot called 41 (there are 40 cells per tier, four floors high, 41 is behind the cells on the first tier, no one can see a blind spot.) and I was in the fight of my young life. I lost, the odds were against me 4 to 1, and I couldn't fight a lick. I lost my hat, jacket and shoes. I went back to my cage, only to find the rest of my stuff, clothes and food, all gone. I looked up and down the tier in disgust and walked in to see if there was anything left. The only thing no one wanted was a box of powdered milk.

But the most important lesson I learned that day and can give to young felons going into the joint for the first time is 'You have to fight! You don't have to win, but you have to fight'

I must have fought fifty times that first year and lost a lot of fights and property, but my skills were improving. I probably spent 3 out of every 7 days in the hole.

It was a big joke with the guards, that they would hold cell 15 open for me. They told me that every time they let me out.

But the hole was cool, it gave you a little stress free time to work out, relax and catch up on your sleep. Because in General Population you didn't dare sleep to deeply or if you did, you might not wake up to greet the new day. In the hole, you could sleep long and deep. Most guys did *just that* for the first 3 days. They just slept, ate and slept. Then you spent the next three days reading the walls. As they are covered in graffiti and crude art work.

In General Population, if someone walked by your cell while you were sleeping, you were aware of it. If they stopped in front of your cell, you were awake. If the door racked open, you were rolling out of bed, shank in hand. It was a War Zone and you might die any day. You always slept in your clothes so you were prepared to do battle at a moment's notice. You never really slept well. (If you think the military has Delayed Post Traumatic Stress Syndrome after serving a year in a war zone… felons live in a life or death war zone for years on end with no R&R and no relief. We don't get counseling inside or when we get out for it. Then you wonder why there is a high recidivism rate?)

If you're in your underwear when the door comes open and someone ran into your room, you might feel more vulnerable against a clothed opponent. You must always be on guard to protect what was yours from whoever was going to try to take it, and there was always someone trying to see if he could take whatever you had. So you slept fully clothed and ready to fight like any good soldier.

You don't leave anything on your bed, when you leave the cell, or someone will pull your blankets up and steal it.

You don't sleep with your head towards the bars or someone might slit your throat. When you stop to talk to someone, don't look at him, watch over his shoulder for his enemies and give him the nod if you see one, so he can nonchalantly turn around to see who is coming. He will watch your back, too. You can't say, "Hey, dudes coming," that might be misconstrued as getting into someone else's business. Etiquette in an outlaw/warrior society must be adhered to closely or dire consequences may result.

You don't talk to anyone you don't know. If someone looks at you, don't look down or away quickly, it is a sign of weakness and will be exploited. But, if you keep looking, it is a challenge. (What do you do? You can't look away, but if you don't, you will have to fight. You give the person a nod while keeping your eyes on him. It is an unspoken greeting, so you both know your eye lock was an accident. It gives you an out. Always look for the out.) Shower with your back to the wall, rinse your head by tipping it back so you can still see who is around you. Never stick your face under the water with your eyes closed. Bring your shank into the shower with you wrapped in a wash cloth. Chances are you won't need it in the shower, but you might need it coming out of the shower if your enemy is waiting for you by your clothes, shank in hand. These are the rules you need to know to survive in Gladiator School or almost any real prison in the USA.

One day, I went to the guard's booth to get some tobacco and matches and there stood Charles Campbell. He used to take ducks to his cell and play cards with them for pushups and if he was lucky and the kid had to do most of the pushups and grew tired Charles would then jump on them and rape them. He was the only one I knew of, in prison, raping men. Now Campbell could fight a bit. He wasn't any one punch fighter unless you counted the 140 pound kids he preyed on that couldn't fight. But because he could fight and he was a major marijuana supplier, he was the only white rape-o walking population. He was just a piece of shit that found a way to make himself useful, so we let him live. Mostly, no solid convicts would have anything to do with him. I say white rape-o because there is a lot of black rape-o's walking the main line, but the blacks don't look at rape as a bad thing, so they don't outcast their brothers for raping. That is a culture thing. Whites see things differently. If you victimize a woman or a child, we view it harshly. If you're a rapist, you better become useful fast or you will die.

There was this big guy, Lewis, who insisted he was going to stomp me out, he was grand standing, telling everybody my days were numbered. He was a body builder and weighed about 240lbs, 6 foot, but he was still looking to prove himself. He was scared in his heart. He didn't have a lot of self confidence or courage (What we called 'No Heart'), so he was looking for an easy victim and at that time I was losing a lot of fights.

Usually, we need a reason to attack someone, even in the joint. I had never even talked to him before. He was just hoping to build his reputation by beating on me. Well, I never have been one to put things off, so I saw the huge dork in the big yard and ran up on him, saying, "If you're going to do something, Lewis, quit talking about it and do it."

He was stuck like Chuck, he had to do something now, or everyone would call him a punk for letting my light ass disrespect him and call him out. (You have to answer a challenge in the joint, it is the rules.) He grabs his shirt where the buttons connect and pops all the buttons off, pulls it open and tried to drop the shirt. As it is passing his elbows, I attacked the big dumbass fool. Now he can't get his shirt back up or down, he is stuck with it around his elbows, tying his arms up. I proceeded to thrill his big slow ass, I thoroughly beat him down. I had him on the ground, pounding his head into the soft turf. The fight continues until I am tired and Lewis is barking, "Ok, I quit, I quit! You win!" So I let him up and he walks away with his buddies. I know they are roasting him for letting me win.

The next day as I was coming out of the hallway on my way to the yard I hear someone say, "Lewis, if you sucker punch that kid, I will break your back."

I step wide of the door's edge coming out of the unit towards the yard, and sure enough Lewis is laying in the cut for me. If it hadn't of been for J.W. saying something, my dumbass would have walked right into it. But now he has new worries, the guy threatening him is ' *A Name* ' "J.W." (A person well known for their clout in the Joint is *A Name*. The way to get clout in the joint is be tough.) He is sitting there in the grass playing his guitar with a little black guy named Michael. Now Michael looks black, but is half Korean and was raised Korean. Michael is another Name, well known for his martial arts ability to kick guys much taller than his 5'5" stature, in the head. I don't really know J.W. except by sight and reputation. I whipped Lewis's ass fair and square. I offer to do it again. Lewis is trying to tell J.W. I sucker punched him, but J.W. says he saw the whole fight, so wasn't buying any of Lewis's bullshit. So Lewis leaves.

Then J.W. invited me to sit for a while. I did, (a little scared and proud to be seen with these two.) and then J.W. said to me, "Boy, you got heart, but you got to learn to fight." J.W. knew Savate (French foot fighting) and Michael was a good Martial Artist in his own right, so my training began.

The first thing they taught me was to run one hour every day. That way if my enemy could fight better than I could, I could out last him just blocking his blows and covering up. Then when his arms got tired and heavy, it would be my turn to beat on him for a while, until he says, "I quit", Then I was to say, "No, you quit when you were tired, now I'll quit when I am tired" and I would continue to pound him down until I was tired.

After I did that a couple of times, word got out through the prison grapevine that I wasn't one to take lightly anymore and that I might be a little crazy. About that time I got the nickname Thor, because of the way I kept fighting and usually with guys that were a lot bigger then I was. But being trained by J.W. and Michael, no one wanted to fight me for fear of what I might have learnt already.

I was gaining respect in Gladiator School and prisons run on respect. WSR was one of the toughest prisons in the country back then, only a couple slots below Walla Walla. Walla Walla was like in the top 5 most dangerous prisons in the USA. Monroe was in the top 10 to 15.

Not too long after that, I shanked my first felon.

His name was Robin and rumor had it that he snitched on his crime partner Andy, so to prove myself to the Lifers Club I agreed to stab this dude. They handed me a lame shank, a welding rod with a wood handle and some torn sheet around it so it wouldn't hold any fingerprints. Then we all went to the movie house that night and I took a seat right behind Robin and when the movie was going good, I drove my shank down through his neck muscle into his lung and it got stuck in his rib bone on the inside. (That's the problem with pointy shanks. They tend to stick in bone and are hard to pull back out.) Then, I tried to pull it out but it was stuck firmly in place, the Lifer next to me whispered, "Leave it, let's go," so we did.

Robin sat there, blowing blood bubbles and twitching. Everyone cleared a space around him so he was sitting all by himself. After about five or six minutes the guards took notice that something was wrong and stopped the movie, turned on the lights, then came and escorted Robin to the hospital. As soon as Robin and his escort were out of the movie house, they started the movie back up.

I was a little shaken but feeling pretty good. I had proven I was a convict, someone to take seriously and maybe fear a little. I went out and got a job in the auto body and mechanics shop and took one of them long skinny Craftsman wrenches and a grinder and ground the wrench into a fine dagger with a blood groove that said Craftsman.

Then I went to the woodshop and had a guy make me a handle that fit the box-end part that I left on the unsharpened end. Now I had a shank that would never fail. I sharpened it with sandpaper and on the concrete floor in good convict fashion until you could shave the hair off your arm with it. (That is a good shank, something you can slice and dice with. I only make good shanks.) Now I was an armed and dangerous convict, and a Lifers affiliate. I could yell, "Lifers up!" and they would respond.

They had no idea of the headaches I would cause the club, but then they didn't really care either.

Because we made the rules, we could change them within reason. You couldn't be a rape-o or a snitch and you had to be willing to fight, win, lose or draw didn't matter. If you lost to "A Name", it wasn't a big deal you got teased for letting your mouth pass checks your ass couldn't catch. If you lost to a duck or ding you really got teased. But as long as you kept putting up your dukes anytime anybody disrespected or challenged you, you showed heart, so you were okay. (To "Show Heart" was to "Show Courage". It means the same thing. If you were a coward there was no place for you in this Warriors Society. We need to know we can depend on you in any given situation. Our life may depend on it and yours defiantly does.)

But in the case of Robin, it wasn't as simple as it seemed. About six months after he was shanked, I was sitting in The Lifer's Office and in walked Robin.

So I say to him, "Don't you have some place to be? Like down in P.C.?" (Protective Custody)

He replies, "Maybe, but I was stabbed about six months ago and I think it was by a Lifer."

"So what?" I said challengingly.

"I just want you to read this." Robin has a thick stack of paper in his hand.

"What is it?"

"My court transcripts and it proves I didn't snitch on no one. My fall-partner, Andy took the deal and testified on me, then got to the joint before me and spread all that bullshit about me."

I read his transcripts as he suggested, and it turned out I had stabbed the wrong guy. Such is life. It wasn't my first "BAD" decision and it wouldn't be my last, as you will see if you continue to read on.

But that meant that Andy had put a false snitch jacket on Robin and had to be taken care of and it wasn't my job.

Putting a false jacket on someone was bad, it meant your word couldn't be trusted, and we do all our business on our word, so your word had to be good.

Andy was the snitch, so a couple other guys took Andy out to the yard and stabbed him 17 times and kicked him in the head and made his eye pop out on his cheek before they left him for dead.

He laid there from like just after lunch until Yard In just before dinner, about 3 hours, maybe. If the guards noticed they didn't care, or maybe they thought he was taking a sun tan. In any case, the guards didn't come into the big yard for anything back then while the convicts were in the yard. They waited until we were "Yarded In" before investigating anything in the yard. During those times, we ruled the big yard and they might not make it out alive if they were dumb enough to come in there. Andy survived, I don't know how, some guys are just hard to kill, I guess. He lost an eye then went to P.C., I never saw him again.

But from this I learnt a lesson, be it for good or bad. I won't take your word on it, that someone isn't any good. You need to have paperwork. If you tell me a person isn't any good for whatever reason, I will then tell you, "Go tell that person that he ain't any good," for whatever reason you claim, Rapist or rat. I will go with you, but in our world "Might *is* Right". You will have to kick his ass if he wants to fight. The Convict Code says 'He has to fight or what you said is true.' So defend your honor or you have none. Defend yourself, suck dick or die is pretty much the law of the land in true prisons everywhere.

When I first got to Monroe, I didn't even like to watch a fight because I felt sorry for the victim. I only fought to protect myself and I was barely archiving that, so I couldn't help anyone else.

But, after I was in Gladiator School for a while and had a little training, my views on fighting changed. I enjoyed watching a good fight even if someone was getting creamed in the first few seconds. I could see to it that the fight ended when one guy quit. Then also, if a second guy jumped in, well, that was an invitation for me to join the battle. Most fights last under a minute in the joint, but not all.

Fights can start over little things, so if you bump into someone or if someone bumps into you, both of you say "Pardon me" or "Excuse me", just to be polite. In fact Prisoners are probably over polite just to keep the peace. That is another rule to keep in mind if you find yourself in a situation like that. Be polite always, you don't know if the man you bumped into just got a dear John letter or if his Mom died. He might kill you just because he is having a bad day and you bumped into him and didn't acknowledge or respect him like he thought you should. Apologize out of respect, not fear. He is your equal, but do apologize.

Chapter Four

Let me say first that I have made some BAD decisions in my life. BAD is just an acronym meaning <u>B</u>est <u>A</u>vailable <u>D</u>ata. A bad decision is one you made with the <u>B</u>est <u>A</u>vailable <u>D</u>ata at the time, and given the same data and circumstances you would likely make the same decision again.

Ok, that being said, I must tell you of another truly bad decision I made shortly after the bad decision to stab Robin. Sometimes I have to wonder how I live with this decision. May a few who have suffered because of it, forgive me? My actions, as honorable as they seemed to be to me at the time… Innocent people have suffered behind this BAD decision. There is nothing I can do to undo it or I truly would.

The stairwell at Gladiator School was a dangerous place even for those who could take care of themselves. It was a blind spot, no cameras, no windows and no guards. It is a spiral staircase. After a while you could tell by the different blood splatters just what happened, if it was a stabbing or just a fight. Kind of like reading sign like the cowboys did. I can't remember a time when there wasn't fresh blood somewhere in the stairwell.

I believe it was in 1977 or 1978 I was coming back from a visit and as I get near the bottom of the stairs I see a clique of like 5 guys kicking the life out of some poor retarded guy. Remember I said only the strong survive? Well, this poor retarded guy is bleeding all over the place. So I tell the clique, "He's had enough."

They probably kicked him down the stairs from the hospital, which is 3 flights up. They are really trying to kill him, so I said, "He's had enough"

One of the clique said, "He's a rape-o."

I respond, "Do you have paperwork?"

"No, but we know he is".

So I repeat my statement, "He's had enough." Now keep in mind, I was involved in plenty of Rape-O's getting cured the only way a rape-o can be cured, a short flight from a high place with a few holes in his hide, but they had no proof, and the Lifer's club hadn't heard about this one. We usually got notice from the guards before the sex offender ever made it to our prison, so I stood my ground.

So one of the clique said, "What ya gonna do?" Now the odds of 5 to 1 aren't good, even my dumbass knows that. I could die fighting these guys myself.

But I said, "I'll yell 'Lifers Up!'" which meant every Lifer in the joint would have come on the run. These five fine warriors would just be a short story at breakfast the next day, then forgotten, so they took the chance to leave and left.

I picked up the retard and dropped him at the Sergeants Office and forgot the whole thing. It was nothing to me. I was always saving some dumb kid from his own folly.

The retard was a rapist and a child molester and worse, he killed and mutilated his victims. So I had made another BAD decision. At times it seems that no matter what you do, it comes out all wrong. I didn't know. I thought they were just killing him for sport. That is a bad decision that still haunts me to this day every time I think about it. If I had minded my own business... but that just isn't my strong suit. I am drawn to protect the helpless like a moth is drawn to its death in a candle flame.

Now, when I got to the joint the only ones being robbed and abused were the white Ducks (New Guys). Not to sound to racist, but if you were Indian, Mexican, Asian, or Black you already had an affiliation, just because of your race. If you were white, you were fair game for everyone including the other whites, because the white race doesn't stick together like that.

After I had made my bones and had a little clout, I started meeting the chain every week and introducing myself to the ducks. I would tell them if they had any problems, if someone robbed them or threaten to beat them up if they didn't buy store for them, to come see me.

Remember me, I am the guy that is taking auto mechanics and auto body repair, so I have access to long wrenches and sheet metal and grinders. Fine shanks are my specialty.

So when it happened, I would tell the victim, "Go get the rest of your chain".

Then I would go grab a bundle of shanks, and look for another chain, if I could find one real easy and tell them go get your chain, "We are rollin".

(Now chain in this instant, is not a metal thing, it is the people who came on the chain bus with you from the Receiving Units at Shelton.)

I would then hand shanks out to everyone. Then tell the crew to follow me in small packs of 2 to 4 guys, don't be a crowd, we don't want to draw heat. The victim and I would roll up to the robber's cell.

Then I would say, "Hey, I want the kid's stuff. He's my cousin or nephew." Or whatever story we had made up to make this my business. Because if he isn't related or from my home town it isn't my business and I can't get involved according to the convict code.

The usual answer was something like, "What? We don't have anything of his."

To which I would have to reply, "I want it back and now or we are coming in." (Now the crew would all be lined up against the wall behind me like they were just talking or watching.)

So the robbers would say, "What, just you two?"

I'd say, "Do you guys have shanks? If not I brought a couple extras for you." Then I would turn to the crew and tell the chain, "Show them." Then everyone would pull up their shirt tail to reveal just the handles of the shanks I provided.

Can't have ducks using shanks, they might actually kill someone.

At this point the robbers were usually changing their story and returning everything they still had.

They were just saying, "It was just a heart check, Bro. You know we were just playing with the kid." But the head of the black people caucus went to the Pres. of the Lifers and told him that they were going to kill me because I was getting into their business.

Gary said, "Ok, go ahead. But you can only send one warrior against Thor at a time. If you send more than that we will riot and not a single one of you will survive." After all, the blacks have never won a race riot to date. Don't know why they keep starting them. The LaRaza (Mexicans) didn't have a problem with my stand. Took it in stride, as if that is how it always should have been. The bikers and Indians always road together and the bikers didn't like it but knew it was beyond their power to change it. I fought a couple bikers and that ended it.

The guards caught wind of what I was doing (they called me "Thor and the Ding Squad") and when they saw me riding in to their unit with

20 ducks in toe, they left the unit so they didn't have to be involved in stopping me. When they saw some duck being lead to a blind spot, they would drop by my cell, tell me and open my door. Out I would go. If I had to go alone, they would show up like 5 minutes later with the goon squad. I was the first line of defense, the delaying action they would use while they got back up. The guards knew I would go save My People. These dumb kids were my people. I had appointed myself their protector while they learnt the ropes. Mostly, it was dumb white kids, but not always.

It was good to be King.

(Ok, it has been brought to my attention that not everyone knows what a Ding is. A Ding is a person who is not yet wise to the ways of prison life, and does things we would not consider normal. We make allowances for them because they just ain't smart yet. Sometimes they make us laugh like a ding-a-ling, sometimes we have to kick their ass to educate them to the right way to act. Ducks are lower on the totem pole, they know nothing. But some guys never got out of the ding stage their whole time. You can only be a duck so long, and only some of my ducks were dings.)

Chapter Five

We had riots pretty much on a schedule. Every year we had the New Years riot, the Fourth of July riot and the Christmas riot. Plus, we had a few random riots in between just to keep things interesting. But those 3 riots you could count on, so everyone bought extra store and stock piled for the riots. As we knew the lockdown followed and the store didn't run during the lockdown.

I made pruno and ran it through a homemade moon shine still twice, so it was like Brandy when I was done. The moon shine still was a little red hotpot with a copper tube melted through the plastic top. I packed the copper snake in a towel filled with ice to condense the steam back into a liquid. The guards didn't have a problem with that, as I made good stuff from tomato paste and raw potatoes with a little bread dough for yeast and sugar. All stole from the inmate kitchen.

They said as long as I didn't sell it to the Indians, they wouldn't bother me. So when my cell was kicked in and searched, they would take my just my snake (the copper tube) or just my sugar or just the cooker. They never took everything. That would shut me down to long, as they often came and got a bottle for themselves from me. I sold an 8 Oz. honey bottle of pruno for 20.00 worth of weed. Then I traded weed for coffee or smokes. As I didn't smoke much then and still don't.

Everyone had a hustle of some sort. But I had to give it to the guards when they wanted some. That was just the cost of doing business. So I was busy preparing a batch of pruno for the upcoming riot, as the guards never did shake downs during the lock down that follows the riots. So it was a good time to run a batch.

Well, the 1978 July 4th riot kicked off on the first of July for some reason. I was stuck in my cell. That is a very bad place to be. You have no place to go. If some guy weaves newspapers into the bars and lights it, the vent in the back of the cell will suck the fire straight into the cell and cook whoever is in it, or since your home alone so to speak, if a bunch of guys get the keys from a guard, before the guard runs… as happened this time… The felons will go down the tiers, robbing cells and killing whoever is home or tossing them off the tier, if it is the upper tiers. We all have like 5 gallon plastic buckets in our cells for washing out personal clothes.

As soon as I hear the riot kick off I hurry up and dump about five pounds of sugar into the bucket, then add about three gallons of water. I then put my stinger into the bucket to get the water boiling. (A stinger is an immersion heater used in prisons everywhere to heat water and are sold on the store or made with two razorblades, one razorblade added to each wire on a plug and a piece of cardboard from a book of matches is placed in-between the razor blades and tied with thread taken from a sheet.) In about twenty minutes I have three gallons of hot syrup boiling. I smash my wooden table, so I have the wooden legs to use for Billy clubs. I have my shank. I am ready for war if need be. Not a moment too soon.

About 30 minutes later some black prisoners have got the guard's keys and are opening and looting cells. When they get to my cell they smile real big, to see me caught like a wolf in a trap. There are three of them. Remember, they don't like me to much because I have been stopping them from robbing the ducks. One hollers, "Hit this cell".

"Before y'all come in sniff the air" (you can smell the syrup cooking).

One of them says, "What?"

I answer, "You heard me, sniff the air, can't y'all smell that syrup boilin'? It will peel the hide right off ya and leave ya with big ugly white scars where ever it hits." I point to the bucket, "I got three gallons of hot syrup cookin' right here. Haven't y'all ever been burnt by syrup before? It blisters and peels the hide on contact." Right then the door unlocks.

One of them says, "Oh shit!" and they all dart back the direction they came from. I can hear them talking. One is saying, "That syrup is bad stuff, I been burnt before."

Then one of them says, "Let's let this nigga go, he ain't a bad one." The other ones agree. But, now they want to know how they are going to get passed my cell without getting burned.

So one of them yells, "Hey nigga, we gonna just leave you alone. We gonna just go right on by yer cell ok?"

I say, "No Problem"

Then one shouts, "Don't throw that syrup on us, ok? Nigga? We just gonna run right on by yer cell, don't throw that syrup, ok? Nigga? You ok wit us, ya hear?"

I answer, "Ok, just go on by then." And they do.

As soon as they are about two or three cells down, I pull the stinger out of my syrup and grab a table leg and my shank and go out, slamming my door. Then go over the rail and drop down to the first tier and head to join the battle in the big yard.

Along the way I see Officer Bolger on Dog side. I run over there and force him to give me his keys. He is just a little guy about 5'6", 120 pounds.

How Bolger got to be a guard during these times I don't know, as most guards back then had to be ex military or something. Big guys, not like the correctional officers of today, woman and pencil necks that can't fight, so they have no business working there. Most of the male correctional officers of today wouldn't make a pimple on a real guard's ass. We understood there was a line between convict and guard back then and no one tried to cross it. We respected each other. Not like today. Bolger was really just too small to have that job. After this riot he was put on graveyard shift the rest of the time he worked there.

Dog side is the blacks' side and he is a white guard. I run him over to my cell on Baker side. The blacks with the other set of keys are nowhere to be seen. They already have been here so they aren't likely to come back. I force him into my cell and make him get under the bunk and pack stuff around him so no one can see him. Otherwise, he might die for real. I tell him not to move or come out until the riot is over. Then I lock him in and give him back his keys. He does as I say and survives.

Officer Bolger is an ok sort. He brings in colored ink and sells it to the tattoo artists, and isn't above sharing his pot with a felon either. But if he had run into the wrong felon that day, he would have lost his life for sure. Besides that he was white and this was a race riot so I had to help him it was the white thing to do.

What happened to start the riot early was apparently the blacks had tried to hedge their bets and wipe out the bikers club a few days early. They had them out numbered and cornered in the big yard, but the Indians saw what was happening and ran to help. Bad Bobby was sergeant of arms in the Lifers club, but was also an Indian. He ran into the blocks yelling "LIFERS UP!" and all the Lifers and the rest of the white boys poured out into the big yard like a tidal wave. The blacks' saw they were in a pincher move and ran passed the trapped bikers trying to climb the cyclone fence to find refuge in the Prison Industries area. No longer were the Blacks bent on destruction, survival was now foremost in their minds. The bikers and Indians were heartened by what they saw and started pulling down the fleeing blacks and smashing them. Some blacks tried to come back to rescue their friends but they then ran into the main force of whites and were trodden underfoot.

This riot went from just after lunch until after dark. The Warden called the Washington state police and the Nation Guard to man the walls. We have busted up the wooden benches and have bon fires burning to keep us warm.

I get out to the big yard and first thing, I get stabbed in the right shoulder. I hit the guy with the table leg and he goes down, then he stabs me in the calf muscle and I drop, he is fixing to stab me in the chest, when a Mexican hits him in the head with a baseball bat. The Mexican then drags me over to where the LaRaza is sitting on some bodies. They won't let the blacks or whites disrespect the dead. The vato tells them to look out for me and rejoins the battle. This was not the Mexicans battle but some warriors are hard to keep off of any battlefield.

One of the Mexicans (Sepida) has some duct tape and napkins he stole from the kitchen and is patching people up, so I get some napkins and duct tape put on my wounds.

Chapter Six

Back then, we had free run of the joint and as I said earlier, we ruled. We had no limit on the amount of property we could have. It was just a matter of if you could hang on to it or not. You could have a clothing package sent from home once a month and food package of store bought items 15 pounds worth every 3 months. Then whatever you could trade for or buy or steal from the guards or weaker inmates and hang on to, you could have. No inventory lists were kept for the convict's property back in those days.

Then the school, Edmunds Community College saw they could make money off of us too. So they sold plants and pet fish through the horticulture class. Guys started buying Bettas' AKA Siamese fighting fish. Then we had fish fights on the tier and big money changed hands during those events. But the fish were the same color sometimes so we had fistfights to prove ownership of the winning fish and big money exchanged hands again during those too.

So eventually it was decided that no two fish that were the same color could fight because a lot of guys didn't want to pay if they thought that the fish they had bet on was still alive. So the fish had to be like one red and one blue or a solid colored one and a two toned one. Then things went more smoothly. I had two 5-gallon fish tanks, a three-gallon drum and a two-gallon squat. I had lots of fish. My fighter I trained with a mirror to hold his breath longer then his opponents, as Bettas' are lungfish and can win a fight to the death by drowning their opponent. Mine was a blue and green guy, a winner.

I fed him live food when I could get it, to include flies, worms, ants, etc. but one day I caught a horse fly and pulled its wings off and tossed it in the fish bowl as I left for work. When I got home my dumbass fish had choked to death on the fly.

Another thing was that if you went to the hole and didn't have a cell partner, the guards flushed your fish down the toilet.... Or so they said, maybe they gave them back to the horticulture class for resale, but the meat of the story is you lost your fish, so guys were trying to not go the hole. So for a while the prison almost tamed down a bit over just having a pet in your cage. It was a good control device for the guards.

Then the horticulture teacher, his name was Mr. Cactus, died of a heart attack. The new teacher didn't want to do the deal with the fish, so Warden Look said, "If you have fish you can keep them, but no more would be sold." Dumb move on his part, as the fish, for the time we had them, kept the prison much tamer then it had been because the guys had something to care about.

Then no more plants were being sold so guys were getting cuttings from each other or stealing plants or cuttings from the counselor's offices. After a while all the fish were gone and the prisoners were back to stabbing, fighting, robbing and abusing each other, life had returned to normal. Or what passes for normal in the abnormal world convicts live in.

So we had it pretty good back then. Anarchy ruled. We lived by the law of the jungle and all that. But it worked for us. We all knew just where we stood. The strong survived and the weak and depraved died.

Chapter Seven

Now when you went to the dining hall to eat, everybody had their own table or seat at a table. All the blacks sit together on one side of the dining hall and all the Indians sat in their section by the bikers, etc. Now I just sat with my friends, not really in the lifer section. Just in the whites section.

Well, I don't know why but for some reason (maybe I looked like a nice guy) the Christians always tried to sit in my seat and keep it. I would come in and put my cups down in front of who ever were sitting in my seat and then go get in line. Now that was the custom, to let whoever was sitting in your seat know that the seat was taken and that he would have to move when you get back. This one time, I do that and when I get back, the guy is still sitting there. I tell him, "Dude you have to go, that's my seat."

He says, "I'm not done eating yet"

So I take a finger and slide his tray off the table on to the floor. Then I said, "There, yer done now, so get out of my seat." and I put my tray down.

He pushes my tray off the table. I swing on him, but my raggedy old corduroy coat has a hole in the sleeve and my thumb gets caught in it and my fist stops like two inches from the dudes face. He then slugs me in the throat. That pisses me off, so I grab him, take him to the floor and start pounding his head into the concrete. He is bleeding from his nose and ears before the guards get there and ask me to stop. So I do. They didn't cuff you up back then. So I get up and they start escorting me to the hole.

Officer Richardson, Officer Carney and Officer Westland are escorting me to the hole. I ask Richardson, "Am I going to get another tray as I didn't get a chance to eat?"

He replies, "Yeah"

So I say, "I get to keep my cigarettes right?" (Because they are Tailor-made cigarettes i.e. Marlboros)

"Nope." It was the guard's whim back in those days.

So I tell him, "Well, then all you have to do is take them."

Then I couldn't believe my eyes. Officer Richardson put up his dukes. I uppercutted him followed with a right cross and he was down in the corner. I kicked him in the ribs. Then Officer Westland grabbed my shoulder to spin me around, so I elbow smashed him in the face, broke his nose and he dropped like a sack of potatoes. Officer Carney turned hiked his skirt and ran like a little girl. Now, by this time I was already in the receiving area of the Segregation Unit. It was a little open shower area with four shower heads and a bench along the wall to put your clothes on while you shower.

Officer Richardson is stuffed into the corner where two benches meet, all rolled up into a ball. There is a cage above on the wall that another guard sits in. He called the Goon Squad. Back in them days the goon squad didn't get all that plastic armor and shock shields or tear gas. They had to come as they were, bare knuckle. So here they come, all big boys with an ability to fight, looking like the front line of the Green Bay Packers. Officer Mull, Officer Davis, Officer Hall, Officer White and Sergeant Clark were the goon squad that day. Man, they just smashed into me and drove me to the ground. They dog piled on top of me, squishing the breath out of me.

They say, "He's done," and they let me up. I get up, brush myself off and kick Davis right in the nuts, hit Hall with a right cross and it is on, baby! They beat me down again. Then they say, "Do you give?"

I answer, "Yep," so they let me up. I get up, brush myself off and kick Clark in the side of the Knee and uppercut Davis (the most dangerous one) in the chin and it is on, Round two! They beat me down again.

Then they say, "Do you give?" (Do you see a pattern developing here?)

I say "Yep"

"NO! Do you really give?"

"Yep, I am tired, I give."

"Nope, he's lying, get some cuffs", so they handcuff me before letting me up.

Now they have to take me to the hospital to be checked out because... Well because we had been fighting. It is up three flights of stairs, all in a spiral with a landing at each floor. Officer Mull (who I might add was a really fair and cool guard, as far as any guard can be cool. You can't trust him anymore than any other guard *as he is a guard*. But he won't set you up on any bum raps or anything and he might let you slide on most stupid minor infractions).

So anyways, Officer Mull and Officer Richardson are escorting me up the stairs. Mull has my handcuffs and Richardson is following… to close, so as we near the top of a flight of stairs I kick Richardson back down a flight of stairs. Mull grabs my shoulder and rams my head into the wall and the rail along the stairs a few times and says, "Quit it, Thor".

I don't say anything. Richardson runs back up the stairs to catch up and just as he catches up I kick him back down the stairs. Mull beats me back into the wall and rail some more. Richardson is coming back up the stair a little slower now.

Mull says, "Richardson, go back down stairs, I can handle Thor and he doesn't seem to like you too much". So Richardson does as he is told. Mull and I continue on up to the hospital.

We arrive and go inside. The nurse comes up, I have a black eye and am bleeding from a few skinned spots and have a fat lip. She exclaims, "Let me have a look at you, what happened?"

"I am fine," I reply.

Mull says with a bit of humor in his voice, "He took on the Goon Squad."

She says, "Are you ok?"

Again, I say, "I am fine."

She says, "Well let me clean you up a little."

I retort, "No, I am fine."

She says, "Are you refusing help?"

"Yep."

Mull says, "Thor, let her clean you up."

"Fuck you, I am fine."

The nurse states, "We can't force him to accept medical attention."

Mull says, "Ok," and we leave. We walk back down the three flights of stairs.

As we get to the bottom, Richardson is standing there just staring at me with his fists clenched and he is breathing hard like he just ran a mile race or something. Now, you know how when you been fighting and your tired, how all that mucus gathers on your tongue? Well, I had been scrapping it off my tongue with my teeth, so it is free in my mouth. Richardson starts to reach for my shirt pocket where my cigarettes are, and I let him have all that spit in his face. Man, it covered like half his face. Mull pulls me around in a half circle so Richardson can't get to me and tells Richardson, "Richardson! I told you to stay away from Thor. Dammit, now get out of the hell out of here and go clean yourself up."

Mull walks me into the Segregation Unit. No strip search or anything. As we are going down the tier Mulls asks, "Are you done? Can I take the handcuffs off?"

I say, "Yeah, I am cool now." So Mull takes the handcuffs off and I sock him in the gut and a right hook. Oh yeah, now it is on, Baby!

The rest of the goon squad comes running around the corner and we are stirring' the gravy. They get me down on my belly, Officer Mull is standing on my back and someone is kicking me in the ribs. Someone else is kicking me from the other side in my knee. Then Officer Davis stomps on my right hand with his Biker Boots and breaks my hand. The pain and adrenaline give me strength, I do a pushup and let one arm drop so Mull tumbles off my back into Davis, and I jump up. I do my best imitation of the Hulk roaring and flexing my muscles. The Goon Squad runs off the tier like a bunch of little girls and slams the riot door behind them so I can't follow.

Now, I am messed up. My right hand is the size of a grapefruit, my left knee looks like a cantaloupe. I am battle torn and bleeding, but looking for another victim. I am angry clear through. But there is not a damn thing I can do about it.

Well, they open a cell door for me to go into, but I am not willing to give up. They have these big concave mirrors so the guard at the desk can see if we are lighting fires on the tier or whatever. The goon squad can see me in it and I can see them, too. But I want nothing so much as to go into that cell and just lie down and pass out for a few hours. But I can't. I don't want to admit defeat. (Never admit defeat, only postponement of victory). So as a way to *accidentally* get trapped and still not admit defeat, I walk up to an occupied cell and tell the felon inside, "I have to take a leak, will you watch and warn me if the guards come back?" Of course he agrees.

I go into the cell and take a leak. As soon as the water hits water they roll the cell door shut. Of course, I yell and threaten them with dire consequences if they don't open the door. Then I sit down, lie down and then pass out. I made a new record. I got 13 infractions for assault on the way to the hole. Unheard of before then, a record I still hold and I still had my Taylor made cigarettes. But Richardson lied he never got me another tray to eat. Well I guess you can't have everything huh?

Now one of them times I was down in the hole, don't remember which time exactly. The Governor was touring the reformatory at Monroe. The Governor was Amanda Ray. I was in R.U. (Restricted Unit, like maximum security back in them days.) So we heard that the Governor was here and started yelling her name over and over in like a chant. "Amanda Ray Amanda Ray "

The guards were trying to not let her come back where we were. But she heard us and insisted on coming back. The guards told her we might spit on her or throw things at her because we did it to them. She said she didn't care. She wanted to see why we were making such a ruckus. She comes back there and the guys are telling her about only getting fed twice a day and showing and explaining to her what fritters were. (A fritter is where the kitchen takes all the food on the mainline and puts it in a blender and pours the meat, potatoes, veggies, desert, etc. into little bread pans and bakes it. That's what they feed us, Fritters. A lot of felons went on 10 day fast rather than eat that crap.) The Governor tells the guard we will be fed three times a day and we will be fed whatever is on the mainline as it is served on the mainline.

I pipe up and say, "Governor, look at my mattress." It is two pieces of canvass sewn around a wool army blanket. The blanket is an army blanket torn in half. We sleep on a solid piece of wood over a block of concrete. I pass the mattress through the bars that are so close you can't get your hand through them.

She looks at Warden Look with this kind of disgust in her eyes and says "Mattresses! And sheets! And pillows!"

So I push it just a little more. "Governor, look at my light."

She says, "Where is it?"

I point to a piece of painted metal on the back wall with some holes drilled in it and a bare light behind it. But it doesn't cast any light to speak of.

Amanda Ray says, "How do you read with a light like that?"

"We aren't allowed books down here."

She tells Warden Look, "These men will have lights and books down here too. This is inhumane." And within about 6 months RU was now not a bad place to spend a week or so.

Chapter Eight

To kill time at night, the prison opened the dining hall to the prisoners in General Population to play cards or chess. Most guys played double deck pinochle (Prison rules), spades or dirty hearts, but a select few played poker for money. Most games are played for something. Be it push-ups, quacks, snaps or money. (Quacks are if you bet me 3 quacks at chess and lose. At any time I can tell you "Give me a quack." you must repeat this cute little rhyme "Quack quack I am a duck, quack quack I can't play 'insert game name' worth a fuck." and I can make you do this three times, once for each quack you bet. A snap is if I snap my fingers and order you to light my cigarette, make my coffee, etc., you must do it.)

I really like playing chess. Now Spike, he is a black Cuban, about 30 years old, well muscled, going bald on top. He has a strong Caribbean accent. He says that he is really too good to play for free. He has to get something for his time.

Well I don't want to get in over my head. A pack of tailor made cigarettes cost .50 cents in 1977.

So I bet him a pack. I beat him in 8 moves. He said, "Hey man, I wasn't ready, let's play again." Now, in chess anything can happen in the first game, while you are trying to figure out your opponent's style, so I say, "Ok" but I am still scared of him because my win might have been a fluke. I beat him in the next game in like 16 moves. He says, "Come on man, don't do me like this, double or nothing" I say, "No problem" because after all now I am playing with his money. But the truth is Spike cannot play chess worth a damn. So after about a month Spike owes me like 180 cartons of cigarettes. At five dollars a carton.. Well do the math he owes me a chunk of money. I don't really want his money, but he is so bad I can't lose. I have tried. I have given him my queen early in the game and still whipped him soundly. Soon, if he doesn't pay me I am going to have to do something to him, and I really like Spike so I don't want to. What I end up doing is like half way through a game; I knock my king over and I concede.

Now Spike is going around the big yard saying, "Aw Thor, he is not a real chess player, Why, I took him for 180 cartons of cigarettes and made him concede the game."

I tell Spike does he want to put those cigarettes up for a rematch. I make him admit he was just winning back what he lost, but it was funny anyways.

On the poker table, I did a real good job of supporting myself. A lot of times, some poor guy would get a little in debt and then check into P.C. (Protective Custody) Well, payment went this way. You must pay on Friday, if you didn't pay your debt it doubled. 20.00 was 40.00 Saturday morning and the following Friday that was 80.00 and it kept doubling every Friday until you paid or got in a fight or got stabbed over it. If on Thursday you came and told your debtor that you wouldn't have the money until the following Wednesday, then it didn't double, cause you had made arrangements. I always told the guys that owed me to please not check in to P.C. I would rather they went to work in the kitchen which paid 120 a month back then and just give me 20 a month or whatever they could afford until it was paid off, but some just couldn't deal with the stress of owing someone money in a place where you could lose your life over a small debt and checked in to protective custody anyways.

One day, Officer Brown kicks in my cell because someone who owed me some money checked in to protective custody and of course gave me as the reason why he was checking in. So Officer Brown decides to play hero and fix my wagon by planting a shank in my cell, which he then finds and writes me up for. I go to the infraction hearing and they have a metal fork with the two center tines bent together and the two outer tines bent down one in front and one in back.

I tell the hearing officer, Sergeant McGowan, "That's not mine. I've never seen it before. Besides you have seen the damage my shank does and that thing there is crap."

Sergeant McGowan says "How did it get into your cell then?"

"Where was it?"

"Under your mattress by the bars."

"Anyone could have put it there like I am going to leave my cell without my shank?"

"I know it's not yours, the infraction is dismissed."

Then about 3 days later Officer Brown plants another shank in my cell and finds it. This time it is a better shank; a steel rod sharpens to a point and infracts me for it. Again the Hearing Officer lets me go but says "Thor, if another shank is found in your house we will have to find you guilty of it.

Well, I have had enough of this bullshit so am going to put an end to it. Not that infractions matter to me they don't, but this is malicious and uncalled for.

So I leave and I go back to Baker side where Brown in working, I get a metal mop bucket fill it halfway with water and go up to the fourth tier. I wait until Officer Brown is walking underneath me on the first tier and I pick up the bucket lifted it over the rail took aim and dropped it. I missed him by inches. The bucket hit the concrete right behind him with the sound of a gunshot and the water jumped out and soaked him. The bucket chipped the concrete. Officer Brown looked at the concrete and then at the bucket and up to where the bucket fell from and walked right over to the sally port, tossed his badge down on the counter said, "I Quit" and left. I went to the hole for 90 days that time, but it was worth it. I never had to put up with him trying to set me up again.

By this time I had done three years for a crime I hadn't committed and I had stabbed a few guys in the process of doing that time, and now this dropping the bucket was the last straw. W.S.R. was tired of my game plan. They figured if I was up to attempting to kill a guard I was ready for finishing school. They were shipping me off to The Walls. (Walla Walla AKA Finishing School, If Monroe was Gladiator School. Walla Walla was definitely Finishing School.)

I didn't want to go. I was scared, Yep, scared. Want to hear me say it again? Scared!

Well, everybody must go through the Receiving Center at Shelton before being sent anywhere else. So while I was there I took a real hard look at the security there.

Now, back in them days they didn't have the razor wire, only barbed wire and it wasn't piled up between the double cyclone fences. It was just a double, triple row on top of the fences in a V shape with one arm of the V pointing in towards the yard and the other arm pointing out towards the street then a curling roll of barbed wire cradled between the arms of the V. The R-Unit (Receiving Unit) yard area was adjoining the visitor parking lot separated by two fences and attached to a breeze way with a top of the breeze way about half way to the roof of the administration building. Then on top of that breezeway roof was another cyclone fence going to the top of the administration building and only a single strand of barb wire up there. Now, on top of the admin building was a tower and of course there were towers at all 4 corners of the yard and there was a rover, (a jeep with armed guards in it) driving around the outside of the yard.

My thinking was they would not fire into the visitor's parking lot. I was wrong. So a friend of mine, Tea, and I climbed the breezeway yard fence, climbed the fence to the top of the administration building before they saw us, and they start yelling for us to get back into the yard. Yeah, right. That's why I climbed up here right? Because, I am good at following the rules and direct orders? Not! I jump into the parking lot and they open fire. I run for a 3-count and change directions. I run for a 3-count and drop to the ground, get back up and run. I make the trees. They don't stop shooting until I am out of sight. Tea didn't follow when the shooting started; he dropped back into the yard.

They got the dogs from the police academy just down the road, but german shepherds are not hunting hounds, so they don't follow a scent like a bloodhound, and are likely to get distracted by some rabbit, deer or raccoon scent. In any case they never came close to me.

I'll bet you're wondering about that rover jeep, huh? It had a lady guard in it. She was firing her shotgun from about 70 yards away. Firing into the air yelling, "Freeze!" pulling the trigger. (A shotgun blast) "Freeze!" and shooting until her ammo was expended.

When questioned, she said she was firing into the air to scare me because she didn't want to hurt anyone. They fired her. My lucky day, her bad luck, I guess. Man, when I was running, it was like it all was happening in slow motion. I saw the tree branches being clipped by the rounds. They seemed to fall in slow jerks towards the ground. The rounds that hit the ground made geysers of dirt that fell back to earth in slow motion. It was totally unreal, but really cool in retrospect.

They fired 87 rounds from what the reports say in about 30 seconds. They didn't hit nothing but dirt and trees. Army Training! You have to love that stuff.

After they quit firing and I felt secure, I am in dark blue coveralls and it is about 3:00 in the afternoon. I rolled in the mud to add camouflage to my blue and started walking. I had been running an hour everyday for 3 years now, I'm not tired and I am not stopping and hiding. Folks that stop and hide will get caught. Plus they got the dogs out. So I find a little trickle stream and just walk in it for a long time. I was keeping to the trees so whenever I hear helicopters up above I can stop and hide for a couple minutes then I get going again. At dusk all sounds of pursuit are gone. I continue through the night.

Sometime during the night I find some power lines and just start following them because it is easier than making paths through the brush and woods. Around dawn I come to a little town, sort of. It is a lumber mill or lumberyard. In the parking lot is a car, with its engine running, no one is around. I walk up to it, get in and drive off. Down the road I hit the brakes kind of hard and a 9.mm Beretta slides out from under the front seat. It was unloaded. I look in the glove box and find a full box of rounds and the clip. I am now society's worst nightmare, an escaped felon armed and dangerous with a grudge to settle for what I deem as society's wrong.

While on escape I thought anybody I didn't know was my enemy. In prison anyone you don't know is a potential danger to you, because you are not sure how they are going to react in any given situation. They might try to rob or kill you with little or no provocation. So paranoia is the flavor of the day.

Chapter Nine

I was angry and thought the State of Washington owed me a big debt. Even though I had a gun, I felt naked without a shank. I bought a Bowie knife and preceded to collect what I felt was owed to me by robbing every store, bar and gas station within 30 miles of my home except one. As a young man, somehow in my twisted mind, I thought the state paid all the businesses back or that the state ran the stores. It was all an 'Us and Them' sort of thing to me.

I can't say too much about them, as they are still unsolved and they have the Three Strikes Law in this state and my real partner has never been caught. Except for one snitch rat-boy friend of my partner. He got caught and ratted me off to save his own worthless ass and tried to rat off my partner too. But he didn't know Leo's real name even though he was friends with my partner. My partner always went by his nickname, which was Leo.

He knows who he is, and rumor has it that he has gone straight and is living Larry Lunchbox's life and that is as it should be.

We did about 300 Robberies in all, in a green 1959 Crown Imperial with a 413 Golden-Lion engine, dual four-barrel carb's, a speedometer that went to 140 mph and a pushbutton automatic. There is nothing like a 'stand out in the crowd' sort of getaway car. But I am a stand out in the crowd sort of fella, so what would you expect?

Well, we did our robberies as a two-man team. The first guy would go into the bar or store and get into a position where he could see behind the counter or around the curve of the bar. So he could watch the crowd and the clerk's hands as the clerk retrieved the money, as the money, back then, wasn't all in the cash register but usually was kept in a bag or a box under the counter. But occasionally they kept a gun there too. The first guy was the insurance. Then I would come in with a hat, dark sunglasses, white tape over my nose and a little eye shadow on my cheek bones, to look like bruising and toilet paper dipped in catsup and dried, to simulate dried blood up my nose. Talking like I had a broken nose to disguise my voice. I would go to buy a beer or a pack of cigarettes and as the clerk opened the till, would pull my gun and announce that this is a robbery.

Then after the clerk gave me all the money in the till I would say, "Don't be a fool and die for someone else's money, give me the bag or box under the counter or I will splatter your brains on the wall behind you and get it myself." If they hesitated I would say, "Is it worth it? What will your family think if you died for someone else's money?" as I pulled the hammer back on the gun.

The whole time my partner is just watching to be sure when the clerk reaches for the money under the counter, he doesn't bring up a gun, and he is watching any customers in case a there was hero in the crowd. If either happened he would pull his gun and tell them to just relax.

It never happened, but it was nice to know I was insured. After I left, my partner would leave and if the clerk asked him to stay and be a witness he would just say, "I can't, I got a DUI warrant and I'm not going to jail just to be a witness." Then he would leave and walk down the street, I would pick him up and we split it 50/50. Then occasionally he would be the robber and I would be the insurance.

But that wasn't the first robbery or two, I did those solo. Man what a scary amateur I was. I was more scared then the poor victim I think. Luckily no one got hurt.

There was two times I didn't even get the money. The first time it was an older babe must have been around 50. I bring a half rack of beer up to the counter and she rings it up, opens the till, I pull my gun say, "Give me all the money!"

She closes the till and pulls the key out and puts it in her bra. Then she tells me to leave.

I tell her, "Look lady, it's not even your money. Give it to me or I will splatter your brains on the wall behind you and I'll still get the money."

She says, "No! Leave now or I'll call the cops."

I reply, "Lady, what is your family going to think when they find you died here over someone else's money and I got the money anyway."

"That is it!" and she dials the phone for the police. I am not going away empty handed, so I grab my half rack of beer and start heading for the door.

She yells, "Bring that back here, you didn't pay for that!"

I say, "No way, lady. I am getting something." She's a sweet, but foolish woman. I know a lot of guys that would have pistol-whipped her or worse, but to me it wasn't worth it.

The second time, it was an Asian. I pointed the gun at his wife and told him, "Give me the money or I'll kill her."

He is screaming at me, "No money, no money! You leave now!"

When I left with the beer he was screaming at me in the parking lot. He was just stupid and I probably should have shot him. It is one thing to risk your own life but to place no value on your wife's life....

But I never thought killing someone for money was worth it. If one cashier won't give me the money the next one will. Now if someone had pulled a gun on me, yes, I would have killed him or her with a quickness. I am an outlaw and a warrior and I value my life above yours.

Now, about this time I hook up with a cute young babe. Audrey, she's like 5 foot nothing, mousey colored long hair, pretty hazel eyes. She is pregnant with someone else's kid and wants to have an abortion. The baby's father doesn't really want her and she doesn't really want the baby. But I say no, I will raise the child. It wasn't an easy thing to convince her to keep it. But I guess she figured if she wanted to stay with me she had to keep the baby. I am definitely pro-life where babies are concerned. As I adore kids. So I let her move in and I help her out in every way I know how too.

My first wife (just a girlfriend then) got to wondering where all the money was coming from. So I stole a line right out of the God Father. I told her that, that was men's business. She ought to stick to women's business of cooking and cleaning and let me worry about men's business. I told her I got it from my people. I led her to believe I had connections from prison and maybe I was a driver or button man. I even went to downtown Seattle where there was a place that sold fake ID that said Mafia Button man on it. It was good stuff. I had one made and showed it to her. I used to pull over next to a nice car and tell her wait here. Then I would go talk to the guy in the car and come back and tell her that I would be out late tonight.

I would usually just tell the guy in the car, "Nice car dude had it long? What did it cost? Ok see ya." Then walk back to my car and get in. she was young and gullible. It was fun.

So life went on as usual. Then she, of course, told my Mom I was in the Mafia, and my mom did a bit of yelling before I convinced her it was fake id and I was just teasing the wife. Then I told the wife, I lied to my mom and it was all real but she better keep her mouth shut if she didn't want to disappear.

So anyway, I wasn't the best guy back then. My girlfriend and I are having a few problems but I don't want to dump her because she is pregnant and I did say I would help her raise the kid.

But another cute babe Sharon calls me and asks if I want to go to the Puyallup fair. She's been drinking. Naturally, I say no problem, I am on my way. She is the opposite of my girlfriend, dark long hair, and dark brown eyes. Not pregnant and built for fun so I run down and pick her up, then off we go to the fair.

Drinking and driving and just having a good ole time. Well, on the way home trying to impress my little honey, I got the car going for all she's worth. It is a 1964 dodge dart I have. We are doing 110 mph when the cops pull us over. The cop sees the beer bottles and I stick the gas pedal under the mat and put the car in neutral and let the engine roar. I tell the cop the gas pedal stuck.

He says, "Son, I been following you for 11 miles and when you were behind traffic you slowed down just fine, but when the road was open you were flying."

So I start pleading that I was in a hurry to get my young girlfriend home on time so her dad won't get mad. The cop was just about to let me go with a warning, but he picked up a beer bottle to toss out of the car and sniffed it and, "Boy, you have been mixing beer and whiskey? You're going to jail."

I am like, "Oh, Shit."

He inquires, "You have any ID?"

"No sir. Just moved here from Minnesota and lost my wallet on the way."

"Is this car in your name?"

"No sir just bought it yesterday."

"Ok. Call someone to come get it and your girlfriend. What's your name?"

"James Lauer."

"Ok, James." He takes me to jail in Thurston County (Cops are just as dumb and stupid as YOU LET THEM BE). They book me and fingerprint me. I spend the weekend in jail and on Monday, I go before the Judge.

I plead Guilty and the Judge says, "Son, Go get a License and get the car registered in your name within 30 days and we will drop all charges, ok?"

I am like, "Yes, Sir." So I am released, I go get my car. Then I call the Thurston County Jail and say, "This is James Lauer. You just released me from the jail this morning."

The cop says, "Yeah what do you want?"

I say, "Well, my real name isn't James Lauer. It's Robert Thorson."

"Why did you lie about it?"

"Well, I am on escape from prison and wasn't in a hurry to go back. See ya." and I hang up. I continued to drive that car, too, until I wrecked it and never got stopped.

Well, Thanksgiving Day rolls around and everyone is at my Brother Doug's house for turkey day (Thanksgiving). They are all watching the football game on TV. I don't know much about football except I am for the other team. Don't matter which team they are for, mine is the other team. Well, their team made a touchdown and everyone went to the kitchen to get some food except my Momma, Audrey and me. So their team kicks the ball off and my team catches it and runs it all the way back.

So I start to yell to everyone in the kitchen, "A home run! They made a home run!"

My wife slaps me and says, "Shut up, you're embarrassing me that was a touchdown!"

I say, "But he ran it all the way home."

My momma says, "It looked like a home run to me."

My wife is thoroughly disgusted with me and says "Just shut up, it was a touchdown."

Chapter Ten

Now any crime you make a habit of you will get busted for. That is the law of averages. So one night my partner, his snitch buddy and I were having a drink down at a bar called the Jig Saw in Seattle and this guy comes in waving a fist full of money around.

Now, on the norm, I didn't rob citizens, I preferred to rob stores, which I considered the establishment. But this guy had a wad of cash big enough to choke a mule. So I made an exception in his case. I looked at my normal partner and gave him the nod at the guy. "Whatcha think?"

He said, "Yeah!!"

I said, "What about yer pal?" So Leo tells his pal who had been hearing us talking about our past robberies, that we are considering robbing this fool who is buying rounds for the bar and spending my money.

The guy is just back from Alaska, off a crabbing boat and is carrying all his cash around, flashing it in bars. He is asking for someone to take it from him. So the rat says, "Yeah, I am game." So we watch as the pigeon is getting ready to leave, we follow him outside; he is going into a dark bar parking lot alone.

I call out to him, "Hey pal, you got a light?"

He says, "Sure," and reaches into his pocket.

At that moment in one smooth move I grab his shirt front and slap him on the cheek with my Bowie knife and say, "Give me the money man or I'll cut it outta you. "

I have to give the fool credit. He didn't just give it up. He knocks my hands up, which makes me cut halfway through his ear before I pull the knife back and way from him and puts up his dukes. He is going to fight. 3 to 1 odds and I have a 16-inch blade sticking out of my fist. Leo is 240 pound of naturally big kid. He picks up the victim and body slams him. Right about that time, a guy in a black Trans Am pulls up, jumps out of his car and charges in the fray. We break and run. (It's the unknown element that you can't account for.) So I am running and I hear 2 sets of footfalls chasing me. Someone says, "When I catch you I am going to stomp you out."

Then I hear "Robert…. Robert Thorson! Help, he is going to catch me." I stop and see the rat boy, Danny, run by me. The other fella is coming up fast.

So I extend my arm with the Bowie in it, flat of the blade towards the hero and say, "Prepare to die!"

The hero stops in his tracks, spins around and runs in the other direction. And he says I know who you are now as he is running away.

I tell rat boy, Danny, if he ever says my name again I will kill him. Then we go find my partner. We head back to the car, but it is surrounded by cops with dogs in the parking lot. They are going to track us. But Leo is right there watching the whole scene, so we signal him to join us. Then I take the boys on a short 'lose the dogs' trip. Everyone walks in my tracks until we jump over the fence. Then we run in a big U shape and go back over the fence. We walk back to where we first jumped the fence and then run back along our track the way we first came and jump as far from our scent as we can and do a similar thing in a different direction then split up. So there are two strong scent trails with all out scents leading to a circle at the end. We leave in three different directions and agree to meet inside a Safeway or some large store where all the other people scents will mask ours.

We decide to walk home except the rat boy. He says he has a girlfriend that lives nearby. So goes his own way. As Leo and I are walking home, we see rat boy going by in the back of a cop car. He had gone right back to my car and crawled into the back seat so he could sleep. Did you ever know such a dumbass? (Dumb people should never take up a life of crime, but they do, the prisons are full of them.) The victim saw him do it and told the cops where to find him. The rat boy makes his first statement and it is sort of good but he still includes my name in it. Then like 2 hours later the rat boy spills his guts on everything he knows and everything he thinks he knows. Trying to save his worthless ass from whatever the cops scared him with. Then he agrees to turn states evidence and testify in court against me and Leo if he gets county jail time with work release.

Mean while, I have no clue what has happened. So I go to pick up my car the next day in the bar parking lot. But it has been towed. I call around and find it at Thor's Towing on Alki Point. I call and ask why it's there and what it's going to cost to get it back. I am told it was towed as abandoned in a bar parking lot and it would cost me 40.00 to recover it. I say no problem I'll be right down. So my brother Michael and my pal, Freddie takes me down to pick up my ride. We get there and the clerk says, "Just one second, I'll be right back, the paperwork is in the other office."

He walks out of the office and about 2 minutes later 5 or 6 squad cars pull up, cops jump out and we are surrounded. All the cops are pointing their guns at my brother Michael with his long hair yelling, "Freeze Robert."

I try to slip out past the cops, but they tell me to freeze too. They check Freddie's ID and send him packing. But me and my older brother, Michael are going to jail. Neither of us had ID. So off to the county jail we went. Needless to say, my poor brother wasn't a happy camper. But so what, he had gotten me into trouble plenty of times, so I wasn't even close to being even with him. To this day he still has done me wrong a lot more than I ever did him, so a week or two in jail was my gift to him.

I get to the county jail and I don't know "nothin' 'bout nothin'". I forget, but I think I may have said I loaned my ride out to someone for the night. (So the life lesson here, boys and girls is: if the cops are asking you questions, it is because they don't have enough evidence for a conviction. Just keep your mouth shut. If they have you dead to rights, they aren't wasting time talking to you, and don't sign away your right to a speedy trial, which will just give the D.A. more time to build a case against you.) But the cops aren't buying any of my story, they already had a statement, and a state's witness. So they book me and put me in a tank. I went through the whole pretense of the justice thing. Had my jury trial, the state's star witness was Danny the rat. Even then, because I didn't talk, the jury wasn't sure and brought back an attempted robbery conviction. 10 more years added to my prison sentence. (Man, why didn't I stop when I was ahead? If I had just shut up and done my time, even if they max me out, I would have gotten like 7 more years to do, 10 at the most. Probably get out in 5 years. But alas, hind sight is so much clearer then foresight).

Well, about this time I got married for the first time, remember my little pregnant girl, Audrey. Well, I married her on February 19th 1980. 9 days before my son Joseph was born. I probably didn't do her any favors making her keep the boy, as I wasn't going to be around to help raise him, but I couldn't let her kill him before he was born. He was born with no thought of the future. I never was one to be concerned with the future. I live mostly in the moment, even today.

Chapter Eleven

So anyway, they send me back to prison. At Shelton Receiving center they keep me in Maximum Security (the Hole). I can see they have fixed the area where I went over the fence during yard. They aren't taking any more chances, I guess.

I see the shrink that told me I was going to be a punk or pay protection at WSR walking in the breeze way. He is walking, looking down at him feet, so I step in front of him blocking his path. He stops and looks up and says, "Excuse me."

I say, "Don't you remember me? I am the guy you told was going to have to suck dick to survive at Monroe." He starts looking around for a guard or any assistance he can find. I watch the fear play on his face for a moment and laugh and walk away. He was such a puss. Looked like Horshack off the TV sitcom Welcome Back Kotter, but had that Jewish nasal whine to his voice like Billy Crystal.

While I am there, they got a surprise for me. One day they say, "Thorson, roll it up, your transferring."

It's not like a chain day and it's in the afternoon. Transfers usually happen in the morning before sunrise. They take me to downtown Shelton and book me for escape. I am thinking, no way they charge you for this. I thought it was just an infraction of the rules or a write up as we called them, but I walk into this jail and it is on the third floor. It looks like something out of the Wild West. Aw heck, one of the lower bars was already sawed out from someone else's attempted or successful escape.

I say "You don't expect this hamster cage to keep me do ya?"

The guard, Officer Glass retorts, "It will hold you just fine."

I say, "Ok." Then to be sure I wasn't going anywhere the guards took my shoes.

That night, I run into a kid named Ged. He has a butter knife he has stolen from the meal trays that the guards don't even know about. I start plotting an escape. I get the knife from Ged and sharpen it in good prison fashion on the concrete floor. Two other kids join the crew in the planning. Now, this is Friday night. (Those two would later testify against us for a reduced sentence. Good criminal help is always hard to find.) Well, Saturday morning rolls around and in comes Tea. He's the kid that was in on the escape from the R-units. He walks in and right away I run down the plan to him. Well... you have to know. Tea is game, so that night we sit in a cell, Ged, Tea, The two rats and me. We get the plan down. I have the knife. Now, I am sure no one but Tea and me believe we will really do this or that it will work. Ged was the Porter here at the jail before getting fired, so he knew where a lot of things were, like the guns and our clothes. He was an important element to the success of our plan.

That night I sat down and wrote myself a tear jerking letter from my sister stating that my mother had been in a horrible car wreck and was on life support and might die. Could I please call home so we could talk?

The next day I waited until the evening shift of guards came to work. Then I waited until it was just starting to get dark. I called the guard back to the cell block. Officer Spooner came back. I showed him the letter and with a cry in my voice, I requested a phone call. Being about 23 years old said, "I'll get you out for a call, hang on."

He went and got the keys. Now, good ole Spooner had him a short ponytail and was just a good ole boy. Back he comes in a matter of minutes with the keys and opens the door saying, "Phone calls." Gills (one of the rats) tries to run out ahead of me. That wasn't the plan. I grabbed his coveralls and yanked him back saying, "The first call is mine."

Officer Spooner says, "Yeah, let the new guy out first." As I walk past, I pull the sharpened butter knife from my pocket, step up behind and with my left hand grab his ponytail then wrap my right arm around his chest, knife at his throat. I say, "Don't move."

Tea and Ged come running out of the tank. I march Spooner out to the doorway where the other guards can see and yell, "hey! Hey!"

The one guard I can see, Officer Glass responds, "What do you want?"

I say "Make a false move and your partner beats me to hell!"

Officer Glass then repeats himself saying "What do you want?"

I demand, "Your guns!" I see Glass look to his right and make a small shake of his head like a "No" signal. "Tell him to come out or I'll gut this mutherfucker right here!" I threaten.

A little female guard peeks around the corner sighting down the barrel of the little nickel plated .38 in her mitt.

"Your partner will beat me to hell if you don't put the gun down." She does.

I tell Tea, "Get the guns."

Tea and Ged run up there and come back with two .357 magnums and the nickel plated .38 I drop my butter knife in favor of a .357 Python. Then I say, "Alright, everybody in a cell."

Now, I wasn't paying too much attention to my crime partners but from what I later learnt, Ged told Officer Janice (the female) that he could now do whatever he wanted to her. I guess she had been giving him a hard time and was the reason he was no longer the porter. She thought he was going to do bad things to her. Not On My Watch! I am an Outlaw and a Warrior true, but Warriors Code and/or Convict Code says 'molesting women is a crime punishable by death'. I will enforce those codes with my dying breath. She was never in any real danger. Don't get me wrong, I would kill her in a gun fight and not lose any sleep over it. Women can be warriors, too. But she would never be sexually molested in my presence.

But anyway, I march the guards back to an empty cell, where they will be safe and lock them in. After we have them in the cell, Ged says, "Let's kill them."

I said, "No, let's not."

"Yeah, I am going to kill them." (Ged was in for a burglary and was going to do less than a year up to the point where he threw his lot in with mine).

I turned just a little sideways so my weapon was pointing at Ged's gut, eased my hammer back and said, "No, let's not." This was my show, damned if I was going to let some trigger happy fool get me a triple murder.

Ged said, "Ok, let's go then."

Then I released all the prisoners in the jail, but we are still not clear, because we have to go down the elevator to the street. I tell all the freed felons that we 3 are going first and we will send the elevator back up for them. They agree. We get in and push floor number 2 button, thinking we can work our way out from there. As soon as the elevator starts to move, it stops. Gills had run and shut off the power to the elevator then freed the guards. We are trying desperately to get the door to reopen and we pry it open about 4 inches just as Gills is leading the freed guards from the cell block. I stick that big ole .357 through the opening and say, "Back into your cell!" The guards run back to the cell and lock themselves in and toss out the keys.

I run up on Gills and point the .357 in his face, hammer back, thumb on the hammer and tell him "Wanna die mutherfucker?" I pull the trigger and let the hammer go forward fast but not enough to set the round off, as there are detectives down stairs.

Then I order all the felons back into a cell. They complain but I am pissed. I declared, "You can't stop this mutherfucker from shutting off the elevator? Fuck you, Lock up!"

Now, we have a real problem. The elevator won't restart from up here. It is a security thing. The elevator must be started from the first floor. It is in case of a riot or escape. The guards can contain it by shutting off the elevator. Hum, imagine that, and all the windows have bars on them. Oh and we can't get to our clothes either, so we are going to have to hoof it in our dark blue jail coveralls, if we can get out. There are no stairs either.

Luckily Ged, (Remember Ged, the porter?) he was sent out to clean the roof a few times, so he knew the secret to opening one of the barred windows leading to the roof. We all go out there to see how far down the ground is. We see it is four stories down from the roof. Too far for the good ole "hang and drop thing", so I head back in to see if I can find a rope or sheets or something to fashion a rope.

Gills, remember the rat, is on the radio saying, "All Cars respond to escape in progress at the county jail! All Cars respond to escape in progress at the county jail!" over and over again.

That little piece of scum had soaped up and wiggled out of that spot where the bar was missing. He wouldn't do that to escape but he would to help out his captures. Well, no accounting for what a rat will do given the opportunity.

I am like SHIT! Ged runs and jumps off the roof lands in the soft grass does about 3 summersaults in the grass and gets up running. I am like no way! Not possible. But he did it. I look around franticly and see a drain pipe made of that red brick looking stuff about 4 inches around. Put my .357 in my pocket and slide down, Tea follows my example. Ged is a lucky fool. We run for about 2 blocks and are totally winded. The adrenaline rush is sapping our wind. I say, "We need a car."

Ged steps out in to middle of HWY 2 and points his .357 at oncoming traffic and a bright orange 1975 Ford Courier pick up come to a stop. Ged says, "Get out of your truck and run punk!" Both doors fly open and two men get out running. Traffic on the other side of the two lane highway is slowing down and getting an eyeful.

So, I yell to Tea, "Stop the other side." He runs across the road and stops the slowed traffic there. I jump in the back of the pickup brandishing my .357 for all to see and yell, "Don't nobody move!" A white 1961 Ford wagon on the other side of the road starts trying to back up and turn around. I point my gun at it and yell, "You won't make it." The Ford stops.

Tea says, "I want to drive," so Ged gets in on the passenger side and Tea gets in on the driver side. The pickup starts frog hopping down the road.

Ged says, "Dump the clutch!'

Tea says, "Where?"

Ged yells, "Just stop!" So the truck rolls to a stop and the two jump out and do a Chinese fire drill, Ged takes the driver's seat Tea now in the passenger seat. Now that little truck is doing about 80 mph down this little highway. I settle in for the ride. About 3 to 5 minutes into the ride, the brakes come on full blast and we are screeching to a halt. Being paranoid and hyper alert, I think it must be a road block as I wasn't watching out front, with my back to the cab, I was watching the back trail. So the truck comes to a halt sideways. I pop up over the cab, gun at the ready. Nothing is to be seen. I think we went through the road block, so I spin around and look towards the back. No cops or road block anywhere.

Tea gets out and tells me. "Come on, let's hit the woods." He tells Ged, "Take the truck up the road about a mile or two and ditch it and hit the woods."

So into the woods we go, in my socks and bare feet. At first it wasn't too bad. The smell of free air beats the smell of fresh air all to hell I want to let you know and of course being the object of a man hunt always makes you feel more alive. So I was feeling just fine for the first half hour or so. But pretty soon the socks were holey or gone and the bare feet weren't used to this kind of punishment. Tea was setting a good pace through the woods. I had to call for a break after about 30 minutes though because my feet were killing me.

Now Tea was, oh maybe 50 yards ahead at this time. So I yell, "Hey wait up, I need a break."

He says, "No way, come on"

So I yell, "I have a .357 with 6 rounds and you have a .38 with 5 rounds. Wanna have a gun fight?"

Tea says, "I'll be waiting right here."

"Cool."

So we sit for about 5 maybe 10 minutes, we sing a few bars of "Band on the Run" by Wings and laugh. We are high on freedom and adrenalin. Then we start on again, because I know we have to break the perimeter. We need to get as far gone as possible as soon as possible. So after a while, it is just dusk now and I hear tires on a dirt road ahead of us. We are making a bit of noise, not thinking we are near anything but woods and underbrush. The tires stop and the search light on the side of the Police car hit the woods where we are.

I duck down behind a fallen log and Tea is right beside me. We can now see the cop out of his car silhouetted by the car lights behind him flashing his light, looking for where the noise came from. So I tell Tea, "If that light hits us, that cop is dead meat, I am firing."

Tea says, "Me too." Right then we heard a couple shots go off in the distance, then some rolling gun fire going off somewhere not too far away. The cop jumps back into his car turns on the strobe lights and is racing down the dirt road towards Ged's gun fight. That might have been what saved his life that night, as he was really searching for something. It was only a matter of time before his light found us. We all know he heard something breaking branches in the woods and wild animals don't make a lot of noise in the woods.

Now, Ged has not done as he was told and was still driving the stolen bright orange Ford pickup. So the cops get behind him and hit the blue lights. Well, you're not going to out run the cops in a mini pick-up for very long. So, he wrecks it and jumps out and runs into the woods. The cops fire a couple warning shots and that's the beginning of the gun fight. Ged starts shooting back. The two cops in the squad car have him pinned down now and he runs out of his 6 bullets. They walk up and take him. Instead of a year in the county jail, Ged gets 65 years in prison and some good stories to tell, but he gets out in like 13 years for good behavior. Well, no one ever accused him of being the sharpest pencil in the box.

Mean while, Tea and I get up and hurry along our way. That was to close for comfort. As, if we had shot that cop, and I would have shot him to stay free. The difference between the cops in the county jail and this one was the cops in the county jail had surrendered. This cop was still on the battle field. Had we shot this cop, the other cops would have had an idea where we were. Then it would have been a whole different ballgame. Once you kill a cop there is no going back. It is kill or be killed from then on. You would be a hero in the joint if you got back, but like as not you would be on death row. Dead Heroes are still dead. You might as well "Hold trial in the streets," because if they catch you, you're going to die anyway. In a gun fight, if you shoot quickly and straight you might live to see another sunrise or two.

So anyways, Tea and I continue our trek through the great northwestern woods, We follow the road the cop was driving on but we are being a little more cautious now. We run across the power lines I had followed about a year earlier, so we follow them. We are moving slow as my tender bare feet are messed up from blackberry bushes, stepping on sharp rocks and broken branches.

About dawn, we see a house in the woods with some lights on. I tell Tea, "I am going to take over the house."

Tea says "No"

"Yep, I can't walk anymore and I need a ride".

So he says he is not going with me.

I tell him "I don't care. I am going to get a ride" I Injun up on the house, crawling along the porch under the sight of the picture window, sneak up to the front door.

The door is open, only the screen door is closed. I test the door handle real slow, it is unlocked. So I stand up, open the door and step inside all in one smooth motion. All I can see is a young woman sleeping on the couch; the TV is on but only showing the test pattern. I look back outside and motion Tea to join me. He comes at a low run, just like I knew he would.

I tell him sit in the chair and keep an eye on the babe.

He says "Ok".

Then I unscrew the bottom of the phone receiver and take the microphone part out. She can call folks, but she can't tell them who she is or anything. We are safe from that angle. Then I shut the TV off and search the rest of the house. No one is there. No men's clothes either. I find a couple blouses that could pass as men's shirts. We roll our coveralls down and put the shirts on. Then I go to the fridge. She has a six pack of Schlitz Malt liquor, The Bull. I take that. I take 20.00 out of her purse, didn't want to leave her broke but we needed some cash too. Then I notice a curtain I thought covered a window actually covered another door. That door was slightly open. I think, oh shit. I move quickly to the door and reach my hand into the darkened room to find the light switch. I flip the switch open and swing the door wide, my gun at the ready. There are three babies on the bed, like a 4, 3 and 2 year old kids. I shut the light back off and close the door. I tell Tea and I take the car key off her key ring, I didn't want to take all her keys and cause her to worry, I just needed to borrow her car for a bit.

Off we go in her green Ford, dressed in girls' blouses and rolled down coveralls. Tea says he wants to go home. I drive him into Tacoma as he directs me to his Mom's apartment.

Then he says "Wait here I'll be right back".

I park at the end of the block his Mom lives on. She lives about a third of the way down the street. I am parked with the passenger door lined up on the sidewalk as I keep watch for cops or Tea. I have the motor running, listening to the radio.

All of a sudden Tea comes out at a dead run for the car. I swing the passenger side door open, cock my .357 and put the car in gear. I don't see anybody after him yet, but he is beating feet like the hounds of hell are on his heels. He dives in and I floor it. Tires squealing and we are out of there. In a second I say, "Who's after us?"

He looks behind us, "No one."

"Why were you running'?"

"Just in a hurry to get back, look I got an ounce of pot and a gram of hash from my Mom".

So I tell him, "Look don't you ever run unless someone is chasing' you. It just draws unnecessary attention and we don't need that right now."

He says "Oh, ok."

So now he wants to go to his brother's house. I say "Sure, I don't have any place to be."

But I know this is folly. They are going to be looking in these places for us. But we go. Again I want to stay with the car.

But he says "Come on in and get something to eat and some men's clothes", so I am persuaded. I go in and get introduced. We have a fine breakfast.

Then we go looking for clothes. Well, it must be said. I am six foot tall. Not a man jack in this family of Tea's is over 5'8", and most are about 5'5", so nothing is fitting. I have on a pair of pants that are 4 inches to short. The shirt wasn't too bad, it being short sleeved. But the shoes, I wear 11's. The best they can come up with are 9 ½'s. I curl my toes and squeeze into them. I might not be in jail coveralls, but I am still a sight to see.

So anyways, I tell Tea, "Look bro, we really can't hang around here with your family. The cops are looking for us. If you want to stay that's fine, but I am going to have to get out of here." So Tea bid farewell to his kinfolk and we are on the road again looking for a place to hide.

We stopped and get some more beer as the six-pack didn't last. Tea knew a place out in Puyallup by some power lines where he used to party. So we went there made a pipe out of an empty beer can and smoked a little pot and drank some beer. Then we try to catch some Zzz's.

I woke up first and it must have been just when the kids were getting out of school or something, as there was a parade of maybe junior high school kids going by in front of the car. Well one kid, a boy, comes back after he already passed us and looks again at the car and takes off at a dead run.

Well, I am here to tell you pal. I was more than a little paranoid at this stage of the game. So I start the car and gun it. I am flying down this dirt path, laying on the horn. The kids are diving out of my way into the long grass on the side of the dirt road. Poor Tea is bouncing up and down as he was sleeping and has no idea what is going on.

He wakes up and says, "What's up".

I say, "I think we were spotted."

He rolls down his window and is hanging out the window, pointing his gun at our back trail as I hit paved road, rubber squealing and gravel flying. We fishtail down the road for about five miles before I am convinced we are in the clear. We head back down to Tacoma. We need more beer and some gas too.

I pull into a gas station (back in these days they actually pumped your gas for you) and tell the attendant to give me five bucks worth.

He goes back towards the rear of the car. Then in about a minute he is back reaching his hand into the car window and says, "Give me the key."

Now, I only have the car key and don't understand why he would need the key. So I grab the butt of my gun and say "Why?" I am about to shoot his dumbass and gun it out of here.

He says, "The gas cap key, it is a locking gas cap"

I say, "Oh, it is my sister's car. She didn't give me the gas key. I'll be back later."

I start the car up and drive away, thinking I'll get a screwdriver and pop the gas cap then go back and get some gas. But the car runs out of gas about 3 blocks away. It is in the middle of the road.

I tell Tea "Come on lets go".

He says, "Want to push it to the side of the road?"

I say, "Nope, it is a stolen car, let the cops find it."

We are on Pacific Highway in Tacoma, by a Skippers Fish and Chips. I go inside and call my Mom. Hey, when you're in trouble and in need of a helping hand, who else do you trust enough to call? You know you can always trust your Mom. So I call Mom.

My Mom answers the phone, I say, "Know who this is?"

She says "Yep."

"Need a ride, Skippers fish house Pacific ave in Tacoma" and I hang up.

I get back to Tea. But I am really crippled up from my barefoot trek through the woods and these under sized shoes aren't helping matters much. There is some construction going on right next to Skippers too. There is a big pile of sand not too far from the road. I hand Tea my .357 and tell him we have help coming but I need to be out there where they can see me. I tell him if a cop car stops, to open up on the door with both guns so I have a chance to get away.

He says "Ok." But in all reality I looked more like a homeless person then a dangerous escaped felon. I was walking on the sides of my feet, in shoes a size and a half to small and none of my clothes fit. Tea is hiding behind the sand, covering my back.

About two hours go by. I am looking for a 1966 Mercury Parkland, dark blue with a white vinyl top, my Mom's car.

Now, my Momma likes to watch all them crime shows on TV. She figures her home is watched and her phone is bugged, so she drives to my brother's house and gets him to come for me. But first she has him go to a friend and borrow a car, get a haircut and go shopping for clothes and food for me.

After about two hours, a dirty white pickup pulls up. As I look at it, the passenger door swings open and my brother says "Robert?" because he is not sure.

"Yep"

"Get in".

I jump in and say "We have to get my partner, Tea".

"No, come on lets go".

"No! He has my gun and he is right over behind that sand pile".

So my brother says "Ok". He pulls around the sand pile and there isn't anyone there. "Where is he?'

"He must have left". The whole time I thought my back was covered, I was a sitting duck.

Tea apparently got tired of waiting or got scared, but in any case, he left. He somehow made his way down to Riverside California. He was living the good life partying and bragging about his exploits. Well some young buck at one of the parties challenged him, called him a liar. He pulled that little nickel plated .38 out and threatened him. Later that night when Tea passed out at the party, the guy he threatened called the police. Poor Tea was in for a rude awakening. He had a good two week run. Last time I talked to him, he had no regrets. He was still telling his story. I heard his story and in it he is the main mastermind of the escape.

But hey, that is His-Story (history) and he can tell it anyways he wants.

Chapter Twelve

Now my brother takes me down to Georgetown, a seedy part of Seattle, it is an industrial area and rents me a cheap hotel room. Man, I took a hot bath and opened a beer from the six-pack my brother had so thoughtfully brought for me. A hot bath never felt so good in my whole life, I tell you. I get out of the bath and there is a tub of Kentucky fried chicken, so I eat a couple legs and pass out. I haven't slept more than an hour since this whole thing began and I am dead dog tired.

I wake up the next morning feeling like a new man. But I'm still paranoid. I eat a little chicken for breakfast, turn on the TV and enjoy the moment. I keep checking out the windows every few minutes and about the fifth time, sure enough, I see a cop car going by the motel. Well, that's it, I run to the bathroom and climb out the bathroom window and start running down the rail road tracks that go though that area heading south. I came to a golf course and called my Momma, told her what happened. That I thought I saw a cop watching the place.

She sent my Aunt Sylvia to come rescue me. Then she sent my brother back to the motel to get all the stuff I had left behind.

Now, my aunt was driving a hippie type van with all the curtains in the windows and flashy paint job on the outside. She had just moved back to Washington from California. So instead of buying the van to make the trip in, she went to the dealer and asked if she could test drive it and take it to her mechanic. The dealer agreed, she went home, took all her stuff that was already packed and her kids, loaded them up and moved. Test drove the van all the way to Washington.

This is the van she is toting me around town in. She takes me out to my Brother Leonard's house in Puyallup and parked her van like two doors down from his house. She didn't want it right in front of his house… just in case. She told me to stay in the van. So I did. All my folks paraded out to see me and bring me food and such. Well, after a bit I got tired, it got dark, so I went to sleep.

I am awakened by someone starting the van. I say, "What's up?"

My Aunt whispers "Keep your head down and be quiet, the cops just left." She tells me that at about 1:00AM, the Swat team and the Thurston county police department hit my brother's house. But since they weren't sure which of the three homes on the property was his, they hit all three simultaneously.

This is Washington, it was raining and the police had everyone in all three houses out face down in the mud, while they searched. Now, they shouldn't even know that my brother lived here or that he was my brother. The only way they could have had any idea I was there was if they had bugged my mom's phone. But isn't bugging phones supposed to be illegal in America? Well, I have no real way to know. But, since I had never been to this place before and there was no record of this address in my prison records. As I didn't know the address… it sure seemed like something unlikely occurred. Maybe my Momma's Paranoia wasn't so far off the mark.

But in any case, they didn't find me there and Thurston County got sued successfully by two of the households. The ones not related to me that had no idea why the swat team would attack their homes in the middle of the night without cause. They got paid. But my brother and aunt lost their law suit. Guess it is one of the hazards of being related to me.

My aunt takes me back into Seattle and puts me up at the Hilton Hotel by the SeaTac International Airport. Then goes and buys me some shoes size 10. I told her size 11, but like a lot of girls, she thought she knew more than I did about me. She buys some red hair dye and a big white cowboy hat with this big feather hatband, and some State Patrol looking mirrored sunglasses. To top it all off, a bright blue wind breaker. Don't want to make me look obvious, do you? You, have to love her, because she is doing her best, but doggone it. A baseball cap, a jean jacket and the right size shoes would have been better. She has me all dressed up like a rodeo clown, but I am safe and free, that's all that counts to me at this point.

The next day she takes me to SeaTac and puts me on a plane to Ketchikan, Alaska. She makes all the arrangements for me to stay with a friend of hers and gives me my cousin Jimmy's ID. Now Jimmy is like 17 and I am like 20, but what the hell. It will do for a while.

So I arrive and my aunt's friend, Gail, takes me home. She has a spare room and my Momma has given me 100.00. So I am doing ok. But I am bored so I go wander around town, put in a few applications for work, looking for a processor boat job or something. I don't find one, but I find a nice little topless bar called the Shamrock. I start going there and drinking. Now I don't realize that in Ketchikan the bars don't close at 2:00 AM and the sun doesn't go down either. So by about 4:30 in the morning I am pretty smashed. The bartender has been being a good friend and making me all sorts of drinks that I never had before. Well, truth be known I had never had mixed drinks before.

Now, did I mention this is a topless bar? There are a lot of cute barmaids that will sit in your lap if you pay for their drinks. I had no idea that life on the outside was like this. So, I began buying them drinks. But after a bit I am feeling like this isn't right. So I start telling these babes, "Can't you find a better job? This isn't a good job for a beautiful girl like you. Does your Mom know you work here?" and all manner of dumb shit like that. Because I just can't help myself. It is in my nature to want to rescue or save people.

The bartender tells me it's time for me to go home.

I tell him "It ain't even dark yet".

He laughs and says "It doesn't get dark here, this is Alaska!"

I am like "Really?"

He says "Yeah, really, look at your watch." Then he says "You can come back when you sleep this one off, but you can't talk to the girls and buying them drinks it a waste of money, so quit it."

I say, "Why can't I talk to the girls anymore?"

He just shakes his head and says "I'll tell you tomorrow. Good night."

So anyways, I continue to drink there and I do talk to the girls but I don't get that drunk anymore, and I don't try to make them any more moral than they want to be.

I spend about a month up there. In the mean time my aunt who has a lot of friends up there is busy telling them all that I am there and that I escaped from prison 2 times and am currently on my second escape.

Well, being a small town… it doesn't take long before I hear a knock on the door. Gail answers the door and it's the police. They say, "Gail, rumor has it that you have an escaped felon living with you. Is that true?"

She says "No, the only one here is Sylvia's son, James, you know him right?"

"Yeah, can I just come in and look, Gail, to settle this once and for all?"

"Sure come on in"

I went out the bathroom window with just what I was wearing and walked down to the ferry docks. The first ship wasn't leaving for Seattle for 3 days. So I go to the Shamrock. I catch one of the barmaids, Linda's eye, and wave her over. I explain that Gail and her husband had a fight and I got kicked out because of it and was going back to Seattle to look for work, but had no place to stay for the next 3 days and did she have a couch I could stay on.

She said "Sure".

So I call Gail and asked her if she could please bring my stuff to the Shamrock and I told her the story I had told the barmaid in case anyone asked. So Gail brought my stuff. I spent three pleasant nights at Linda's house. Then she saw me off, and on to the ferry I went. Back to Seattle and my wife and son.

On the ferry, I meet this young lady, never learnt her real name, she went by Cricket and was on her way to Beaverton, Oregon with her two younger siblings. Since we were both sleeping on deck, no cabin, we only did the flirting thing. But Cricket sure was sweet and kept me entertained on my trip back down to Seattle.

The ferry was arriving early in the morning after the third day. Now being a little paranoid, and not wanting her to get hurt, I told Cricket the whole story just before the boat pulled into the Seattle docks. I didn't know if the cops in Alaska had found out I was on a boat and had the cops in Seattle waiting. So I told Cricket to stay back from the boarding area until I was gone. Then I went to try to be one of the first people off the boat. There wasn't anybody waiting, so I was on my way to my Momma's house where my wife was staying with my new born baby boy.

Now while on the ferry I picked up a cheap pair of binoculars, the kind that fold into a little tin case. I sat on a hill overlooking my Momma's house until dusk. It took me only an hour to make it there, but I didn't try to go in until it was getting dark and after about 8 hours of watching the house, I was sure nobody but me was watching it.

But even so, I walked around and down the alley and came in the back door. You can't be too careful, because, if the cops had the neighbors watching the house, I wouldn't have noticed that.

So I walk in and of course everyone is in a panic. No one knew I was coming. Well, just the fact that a full grown man has appeared in the kitchen was probably enough to unnerve the two women a bit. So my Momma asks why I am here and I explain that her sister was doing a little bragging and made Alaska too hot to stay.

So my Momma says "Well, you must be hungry." She and Audrey set about digging out some leftovers and fixing me a meal. But my Momma is saying, "Well, you can't stay here more than a night. Don't know when the cops will be back and they might be watching the house this very moment."

So I played with my son, and spent the night with my wife. Then the next morning, my Momma gave me another set of ID and took James's back. Guess my aunt wanted it back. So now I had my older half brother's ID. Then I was down the road to the bus depot and on a greyhound headed for Minnesota.

Chapter Thirteen

Last I had heard my Dad lived there. He had left my Momma when I was three. I had seen him a couple times since then. But truth is we never really got along real good back then. He had ideas on how I ought to act and I never was one for toeing the mark. So we would bump heads mostly. But I thought maybe since I was in a bit of trouble he might see his way clear to helping his son out. After all, he didn't even know he was a Grandpa.

Well, on the bus I meet a girl named Kat, a nice young black couple and another young guy. At every bus stop, we all would get off, buy some beer and smuggle it back on. We are drinking and enjoying ourselves. But not getting to rough and rowdy. We were just having a good time. As we are going through Montana there is an electrical storm going and the lighting is hitting the ground all around us. It is awesome. One bolt hits the road right next to the bus and made a sound like a .44 pistol shot. That made Kat want to sit a little closer and I wasn't opposed to that. She was maybe 28 years old, long beautiful dark hair, a ready smile and a wonderful sense of humor. She was about 5'8", 130lbs, with all the right curves in all the right places. The other single guy was a blonde and I think he was only like 19 years old. The black couple was in their early twenties and had their 3 year old daughter along. We made a fine bunch of happy travelers.

So, we get to Minneapolis, and here is where we split up. The blonde kid is going to Chicago, so will be getting back on this bus. But Kat is going to Kentucky and the black couple is going to Mississippi. So they will be traveling together still, but on a south bound bus. We all go into one last bar together, the 19 year old too. In Minnesota the drinking age is 19. So we had a beer guzzling contest. It was just us guys. It's a man thing them poor boys never stood a chance. Then we all bid each other fare well, and I leave our happy little group to see if I can find my long lost father.

I grab a phone book and start searching. No such luck. But I find my Uncle Ned's phone number. So I give him a ring and he says my dad is down in Texas with his seventh wife. (Facts are my Dad had about 3 different 7th wives that I know of. I don't think he could count above seven.)

But my Uncle Ned says, "Come on over, I will put you up until you get a job."

So, I go over there and I sleep on the couch. Now, after I am there about 3 weeks or so, I guess my Uncle remembers or finds out I had been to prison. Then he asks me about it.

I tell him the truth. "I just got out Uncle Ned, and I am trying to get my life back together. I have a wife and son to look out after."

He says, "If I call the police department and tell them you're here what would happen?"

I am thinking you'll never make it to the phone. But I say, "Go ahead I am off parole and everything"

"Well, I am going to think it over, but I think you should turn yourself in."

"Uncle Ned, I am not lying' to you, I am out for good." And I meant it. I was not trying to go back.

Nothing more is said about it. He just looked at me. But I knew the jig was up. It was time for me to move on.

About 3:00 AM, I had my stuff packed and left the house. I headed north to Canada. I have relatives on my Momma's side up in Sioux Lookout, Ontario. I hitchhike up to International Falls, MN. I tried to cross the Canadian border with my brothers ID and my back pack. Well, that didn't work to good. I was broke and didn't have a dime, couldn't say just exactly who I was going to see or what their address was. So I was denied access, bummer deal.

I decide to go to California, I start hitchhiking down Highway 53 to Duluth, then down I-35 South. Just as I am passing through Minneapolis again, not too far from Bloomington, I meet a fellow hitchhiker. He is about 14 years old. I ask him where he is headed. "California". I ask him why and he says he wants to see the ocean. So I tell him he can travel with me. If we get stopped, he is my kid cousin and I am taking him out to California for his father's funeral. That his parents are divorced and his father was killed in a car wreck and we are too poor to travel any other way. He says cool. So we start traveling together. We catch a ride and it takes us into Des Moines, Iowa. We get dropped off right on the freeway where I-80 crosses I-35. We run down the hill to the over pass and stick our thumbs out.

While we are standing there I notice a little marijuana plant growing not too far from where we are standing. I step over there and pick it. Then from my new vantage point, I can see 3 more plants. So I think someone must have shaken their bag out when the cops were pulling them over. I go pick those other three plants, too. Now I can see into a hidden vale where there is a field of marijuana taller than my 6 foot height.

I am like "Oh My Gawd!" I start dumping my clothes out of my duffel bag and picking just the leaves. Man, this pot has the red hairs and smells awesome. Me and the kid are singing that Cheech and Chong song about "No stems no seeds Acapulco Gold is some badass weed". By the time we are done stuffing my duffel bag, it is just turning dark.

We go back down to the freeway and stick our thumbs out. The first car to pull over is a state trooper. I am like "SHIT!" here I am on escape with a runaway kid and a duffel bag full of weed. Could it get any worse? It's illegal to hitchhike on the freeway to boot. The cop gets out of his car and asks us for ID. I give him my brother's ID and start running my story down on him and my Uncle Robert dying and my cousin, Robert's only child, wanting to go to his father's funeral in California. The damn Kid starts crying. It was priceless. The cop starts saying it is not actually legal to stand here but he will pretend he didn't see us and if we are still here in an hour he will have to give us a ride to the next on ramp.

Just as the cop is pulling out, a hippy type van pulls in and says "Jump in".

We do and as we are taking off, the hippy says "What was that pig bothering you for?"

"For hitchhiking on the freeway."

"If it ain't one thing it's another, always bothering someone for something I guess."

We all settle in for the ride. The hippy breaks out a six-pack of beer and passes them around.

He drops us off in Omaha, Nebraska. We go to a truck stop and get some coffee. I have been telling this kid my whole story. So he says "Have you heard that song Renegade by Styx?" I say "No". So he goes to the juke box and they have it. He plays it. I totally relate. I now have a theme song.

There we catch a ride in the back of a pickup truck, all the way to Las Vegas, Nevada. It was the summer of 1980. There was a heat wave going across the Midwestern states. So I pulled my shirt off to get some rays and traveling in the back of a pickup was great. The wind keeping you comfortable and drying the sweat before it got bad. So I took a little nap. I woke up blistered from forehead to belt line and from knee to toes. Yeah, I took my shoes and socks off too. Man,

I was in bad shape. The driver saw this when he pulled over for gas. The kid just sat and watched me burn. I was a little ticked off at that, but he was only 14. Not the smartest of ages to be.

The driver gave me some sun-block. I had never heard of such a thing. It was yellow and greasy. But I put it on and put my long sleeved shirt back on. About this time that marijuana was dried up pretty good so I got some rolling papers and rolled up a joint, a big fat joint. It did nothing. So I rolled another, still nothing. No way! I had heard of Nebraska No High pot before but didn't really believe in it. Well now, I had a duffel bag full of it. But I figure no big deal I will just buy a bag of good weed for folks to test smoke the pot and sell the Nebraska No High to them. I'll still make a killing. Back then an ounce sold for like 60 bucks. I would cut them a deal, sell it for like 50 an ounce. That's the plan. All we have to do is get to California and buy some good weed.

So, on the freeway on-ramp we sit. With me, sitting in the shade and the kid standing out in the sun with his thumb out. A U-Haul truck stops, says he is going to San Bernardino if we want a ride, but we have to ride in the back. Well, now this is one of them big trucks with the door in the back that rolls down and locks. But the driver says he won't lock it with us in there, in case it gets to hot we can open the door a little bit. We did open it just about 4 inches or so as soon as we started moving. But to me this was heaven. I had it made in the shade so to speak. I still hate the sun to this very day.

We get dumped off in San Bernardino. I used to live in Fontana, not 10 miles from here. So I hitch a ride down Foothill Blvd and turn down Beech Street to my old girlfriend, Jane's home. Well, she has grown up and moved away, but her momma was still there. Norma took me in and nursed me a bit. She made me go sit in a cool bathtub of water for a bit. Then she doctored me up.

While I was there, I called my good time buddy and cousin Steve to come get me. He lived in Imperial Beach, California, about 110 or 120 miles away. But he was good family and he came for me. He brought his soon to be wife Nancy along with him. She was a sweet curvy little babe he had picked up in Minnesota and drug out to the California fun. We all have deep roots back in Minnesota.

Now, at this point I was getting fed up with the runaway. So I did a bad thing and told him this is where our paths part. I still feel guilty about that. Never saw him again. The Sims would have let him stay. I was sun burnt and blaming him more than a little bit for not waking me before I blistered. I don't know if he made it to the ocean or not. I hope he did. We didn't see him on the freeway on ramp when we headed home.

Chapter Fourteen

Now, I had been traveling for a few days and I was a little tired. So I crawl into the backseat and pass out. I wake up and I see we are in real slow moving traffic.

I say, "Where are we?"

Steven replied, "Tijuana, we are in the line going back to the U.S. I just bought some gas because it is cheaper over here."

"No way! Man, I have about 2 pounds of the most kick ass weed you ever saw in my duffel bag"

"Man, don't even play like that!" Steven says a little panicked.

"Man, I am not playing dude, here look." I pull the duffel up and open it up so he can look inside of it.

"Oh my God, what are we going to do?"

"What can we do, we gotta dump it"

Right then a Mexican peddler comes up to the window with a handful of bouquets of flowers, and says, "You buy flowers for the Beautiful Senorita?"

Steven yells, "No! Get the hell away from my car!" The poor Mexican guy is surprised by the venom in which he is addressed but leaves.

Steven says, "Where?"

I reply, "There's a garbage can right over there." There are garbage cans spaced every so often between the lanes.

"Keep the car going," he takes my duffel and goes to a garbage can and starts shaking it out.

I yell, "Steven, just toss the whole bag in the garbage and get back in the car." There is no sense risking a Mexican Prison for some crumbs in the bottom of a bag, if we aren't going to risk it for a full bag. Because it really doesn't matter, you go to prison down there for a joint or 100 pounds. Rumor has it Mexican Prisons really suck.

So, anyways, we make it back to America and to Steven's apartment, right across the street from the beach, all the sun and sand. (I hate the sun, did I mention that? Proud knuckle dragging, club carrying, cave dweller is what I am.)

Now Steven is working as a car sales man. Apparently, he's not doing real well. He is paying the bills. But we have to go to gas stations and steal toilet paper because he isn't making enough money to by all the necessities of life. Now we are going through a lot of toilet paper. Like a roll a day or so it seems.

So I confront Nancy and say, "What is happening to all the toilet paper? I am not using that much toilet paper." Figuring girls are wasteful with such things, she has to be the reason we are stealing so much. It's kind of embarrassing to go to the bathroom, just to steal toilet paper so often.

She says, "Steven uses it".

I am like, "He can't be using that much".

She answers, "He puts a layer of toilet paper down on the water before sitting to take a dump."

I am like, "No way, why would he do that?"

She says, "Ask him."

So when Steven gets home from work. I say, "Hey Steven, do you put a layer of toilet paper down in the toilet before you take a dump?" thinking he is going to deny it. But heck no, he wants to talk about it like it was a work of genius to figure this out. So he says "Yeah?"

"Why? That's pretty wasteful."

He says, "Have you ever been taking a dump and had the water splash up on to your butt?"

"Yeah Occasionally."

"Well if you put that toilet paper down on the water first, that won't happen".

"Ok"

Case closed. My cousin is a fruit cake so we continue to steal a lot of toilet paper.

Now, Steven lived in an upstairs apartment, and after I been there a bit he wants to learn to fight. So I start showing him some moves. A few parlor tricks, nothing too complicated for his simple mind. With the falls, the neighbors downstairs are complaining. So we go across the street to the soft sand of the beach.

Nancy comes along in her swimsuit to distract us. She is a little thick but a damn good looking woman.

After I am there a few weeks, Steven starts thinking Nancy and I are having an affair. When he comes home from work, he shuts his car off half a block down and coasts into his parking lot. When we see him, we do little things to act guilty like slide away from each other on the couch. Just because he slept with my ole lady Vicky when I first got busted and sentenced to prison, he thinks I must be as low down as he is.

What a dumbass. Pretty soon it ticks me off. Not that I wouldn't have slept with Nancy if she wasn't his ole lady. She was hot, but I wasn't trying to cause any problems. So I get pissed off. I rip Steven off for his backpack, and some other things, I forget what now, Sunglasses. Just some little dumb shit stuff like that.

He calls my mom and whines about it so she sends him a little money to cover the things I took.

Chapter Fifteen

Then I leave and head back to my wife and son in Seattle. After all, the reason I escaped was to be with them. I love my wife and son more than anything in the world, so I hitchhike back up to Seattle. By this time I have new ID. My brothers ID was no good in California as he had warrants down there I guess. (It may appear to the reader that I come from a Family of Outlaws and that would not be far from the mark.)

Now I have a whole new identity, of a cousin that was given away for adoption by my Aunt Gerry. She gave away her whole family back in the 50's because her new boyfriend wouldn't marry her with another man's children. So I have some fresh clean ID, and it was real ID, not some fake stuff. Well, a birth certificate anyways. I go get a library card and then send away for my new SSN. Then I use that to go get a Washington State ID card, plus an Indian card as we are all part of the Oneida Tribe.

I am living in Tacoma. A place my mom got for me and my family. Audrey is on welfare and I am selling vacuum cleaners door to door. Well, that's not working out to good. Audrey ends up pregnant again, so I am selling plasma down at the blood bank and doing whatever I can to make a buck legally. But I am not good at that as I had never done things legally before. So it is all a new ball game to me.

One of her friends moved in with us and was suppose to help out with the rent. Pam and her boyfriend were both working, but they were so weird. They would hide their food out in the car, and come inside and eat ours. Pam came into some big money and she was moving out, without a thought to paying us anything. They had stayed with us for about 2 months, so I just took 200.00 out of her purse. She didn't even notice it missing. She had a few thousand and was spending it as fast as she could. Her mom took a big chunk of it from her right after I took the two hundred. Since she wasn't keeping track of her money very good, she probably thought her mom took it.

Then one day I am looking out the window of the duplex we are living in and I see two motorcycle police parked outside. Now, I live right across the street from a biker club house. I know this because there are always like 4 or more Harleys parked outside. I don't think about this. I figure they are here for me, so I go up into the attic. About 5 minutes later I hear Audrey knocking on the attic panel.

I call, "Whatcha need?"

She responds, "Can the neighbor from downstairs come up there with you?"

"Sure."

When he gets up there I ask him why he is up here. He says he is on escape from a California prison. Hum, imagine that. What are the odds of that happening? The only two guys in Tacoma on escape living in the same house.

In about 20 minutes the motorcycle cops start up their bikes and leave. I have no idea why they were there. Maybe they were just taking a break. The house across the street was a biker's club house, so maybe they were just checking out the Harleys all parked out there. They sure did give a couple escaped felons a thrill that much I can tell you.

Later that day I head to my mom's house. I end up going out drinking and shooting pool with my brother Michael. We get back around 11 or 12 at night.

Now Michael owes me a little money. I ask him for it before heading home. I know he just got paid. He pulls out a handful of coins maybe a dollar and a half in quarters, nickels and dimes that he tosses on the table. Proclaiming "That's all you get"

I counter, "Boy you better pay me, don't make me take it from you" and we both stand up.

My Momma rushes between us and says, "Come on now, No fighting." She knows we are the type to try to beat each other to death if we can.

Michael grabs Mom by the arms and pushes her into a chair.

"Git outta the way, old woman," he yells.

I am shocked and yell "You put your hands on your Momma?" then I hit him hard, right in the mouth.

He shoves me hard and the coffee table is right behind my calves so I fly over it and land with my legs on the coffee table, butt on the floor and my back against the couch and he straddles me and starts swinging haymakers. I uppercut him in the nuts, He steps back and I get up. I pop him a couple quick jabs in the mouth and he rushes me. I fall back against my Momma's 20 gallon fish tank and now I have to try to keep from crushing my mom's pets and fend Michael off at the same time. He tries to jab a thumb in my eye. I grab his hand and get that thumb down where I can get it into my mouth and between my molars and bite down until I heard an audible crack. He is cussing but trying to get away. I kick him hard on the side of the knee and he goes down. I pounce on him and lock my knees just above his hips and I am sitting on his belly, just drilling his face with punches. He is wiggling and bucking, trying to get away. We are moving along the floor but he can't throw me off of him. Somehow we managed to work our way into Momma's bedroom where he is trying to pull himself under her bed. He has his face under there so my target is gone. So I have switch targets and am now trying to crack a few ribs.

All of a sudden, I am airborne. Flying backwards, I hit the wall across the room. My oldest brother, Doug, has arrived. He lives two blocks away and his gold 1972 Monte Carlo SS 400 small block with the white vinyl top covered the distance in less than a heartbeat.

So now there I lay and his eyes are on me.

"How dare you fight in your mother's home," he bellows.

I say, "He started it!" No one in their right mind wants to piss off Doug. He has been a mechanic all his life and is strong as an Ox. He is about 5'9" 180lbs and built like at Irish Brawler. He has piercing blue eyes topped with coal black hair and the Indian skin tone.

"Go get into my car" he barked

I do, no thought of arguing passed through my head. I am pretty sober by now. So I go outside and there is the Monte, running, in the street. He didn't bother to park it. The driver's door wide open. I walk around to the passenger side and get in. Now, the dome light in the car is on because the driver's door is open.

Pretty quick here Michael comes. He is acting like he is looking for me, under bushes and in places to small to hide a human in. He is not really trying to find me, but he is making a big show of looking for me. Doug comes out and heads for the Monte.

As soon as Doug gets into it, all of a sudden now (since Doug is there to protect him) Michael can see me with no problem. He runs into the street in front of the Monte. My elder brother rolls his window down and tells Michael, "Get outta the way or I'll run you over!"

Michael does his best impression of the Hulk a couple times complete with a roar and flexing his thin muscles, in the headlights.

Doug floors the Monte and it jumps ahead so fast Michael doesn't stand a chance of moving. As the Monte's bumper connects, Doug hits the brakes. Michael goes flying and lands on his butt about 6 feet in front of the Monte.

Michael gets back up and does his Hulk impression again. Doug says, "This time I am not going to stop, so get out of the road," and floors it. Michael jumps off to my side of the road and slugs the window on the passenger side as hard as he can as we go passed. It sounds like the window shattered. Doug slams on the brakes and opens his door. Michael does the ninja thing, disappears into thin air, vanished, no sign that he was ever there.

Doug asks without looking in my direction "Is my window broken?"

"Nope," I reply.

Doug grumbles, "Someday I'm gonna hafta kill that kid."

Doug takes me home to Tacoma.

Well, now I am without a car as mine is parked in front on my momma's home, so I have to wait a couple days for my mom to visit and go home with her to get my car.

On the way home from mom's I get a flat tire. I fix it and don't think any more about it. Then my car starts making a shimmy sound in the front end and I can't figure out what is wrong with it. I take it over to Leo's house. I have him take a ride with me. He says "Pull over!!" as soon as we get up to speed. We get out and all my lug nuts are loose. A couple lug nuts are all the way off and caught in the hub caps. My tires are fixing to fall off. I go back to my Momma's house and say, "Where is Michael? I am going to kill him."

My Momma says, "What for now?"

"He loosened all my lug nuts on my tires and tired to kill me"

"Uh huh, that wasn't Michael, Michael slashed all your tires but Doug fixed them."

Now I am Pissed. Doug tried to kill me. Doug has been a mechanic since he was 13 and I was 2, so he didn't put the lug nuts on backwards on accident, and that was what the problem was. Now I am pissed clear through. I go look at my tires more closely and sure enough the side walls on three are slashed. Each has like 3 or 4 plugs stuck in them side by side. Besides being illegal, it is dangerous. Your tires may blow at any time under normal driving, but especially under hard driving. My car only has two speeds "Fast as I can go and stop!"

I go smoking tires down to the gas station that Doug works at and shout, "Hey, mutherfucker, what's your problem?"

Doug says, "Slow down, what's the problem?"

"Mutherfucker, you put my lug nuts on backwards?"

"Nope, I plugged the tires after Michael slashed them, but *Michael* put the tires and lug nuts back on."

"You plugged the sidewalls?"

He chuckles and says, "And did a pretty good job of it too. But that's not going to hold. Go behind the station and look for four matching 15 inch tires with some tread on them or two sets of two matching tires with tread on them and we will fix your tires right, ok?"

That's what I needed to hear. I was all good with it then. Doug explained Michael probably didn't put the lugs on backwards on purpose. He just is a dumbass and don't know shit 'bout cars. So I decided to let Michael live.

Well, I only stayed in Tacoma until I quit selling vacuums. I wasn't very good at that. My mom got me another place closer to her in Southpark.

Audrey loved to read them scary books. She had me reading one called "The Orphan". Don't know who wrote it, but it was scary.

So here I am in the front room, reading this book. My son's little rocking chair is sitting right beside my chair. All of a sudden the windows rattle and the chair starts rocking all by itself.

I yell, "Audrey!"

She answers from the kitchen where she is washing dishes. "What?"

"Come here!"

She looks into the front room at me with my feet off the floor, and I point at the rocker, still rocking and said "Look!" (I point at the still moving rocking chair).

"You can put your feet down Silly. It was just an earth quake"

Man, I thought for sure the ghosts had arrived.

We only lived there for about a month, and then we thought it would make our money go farther if we just moved in with my momma. So we did. Yep, I was living at home while on escape, not the smartest thing. But the cops hadn't been there in a couple months and it had been over four months since I had escaped.

I was having a real problem getting a job back then, but then maybe I wasn't looking real hard either.. With my mom working and Audrey collecting welfare, I didn't really need to work.

Chapter Sixteen

Well about this time, Michael and I spent most of our free time drinking, cruising around in my car and having fun. Michael had a powder blue 1959 Plymouth Belvedere that he was real proud of. It had the old push button automatic transmission, but the starter had gone out. Mom gave him the money for a new one. He told her he wanted to look for work but couldn't because he had no way to get to work. She gave him the money and he bought the starter, but Michael is not a very mechanically inclined sort of fella, so for a week he is waiting for Doug to come fix his car.

Now a starter is like 3 bolts to take it off and 3 bolts to put it on and they are easily accessible on those old cars. I didn't know he had the starter, but he complains to me that Doug is taking his time about fixing his car. I tell him get the part and I can put it on for him. He says he has it. We go outside and I see he does. I crawl under his car and fix it for him. In like 20 minutes I have it running.

He says "Let's go"

"Where to?" I ask

"The bar"

"Ok"

We go pick up Grandpa Larry. He isn't any relation to us, just a drinking partner of Michaels. He sells pot to support himself and is always willing to smoke a little with a fella. So that makes him a popular drinking buddy.

We go out, hitting all the usual biker bars and getting drunk and high. Grandpa Larry is doing ok with his sales, so he is buying pitchers of beer. Well, I get to drunk so I head out to the car and crawl into the back seat barf my guts out and pass out.

I wake to Michael driving in the rain and all over the road. He is playing with the push button automatic. I hear Michael saying "One, Two, Three… One..." and the tranny downshifts with a whine and the car spins on the wet pavement, "Two..." and the car straightens out a little "Three..." the car surges ahead. "One... Oh Shit!" I look up and see we are headed right into a concrete telephone pole. I duck down just as we hit the telephone pole with enough force to throw me into the back of the front seat and break the steering wheel where Michael hit it. Grandpa Larry hit the metal dash and dented it with his head.

I jump out and run around to the front of the car. I can see the driver's wheel is bent so the hub cap is facing the earth and the engine is sideways. The fan can be clearly seen through the wheel well where the fender is all crushed. I grab the driver's door jerk it open and tell Michael, "Come on we have to go!"

He is turning the key and the starter solenoid is clicking.

I say "Come on, Bro, we have to go. The car is dead".

Michael says "No, it will start, just give me a minute" he is chanting "come on baby, come on baby, come on baby," as he turns the key.

I tell him "No, bro, the engine is smashed. Get out and look." So he does.

Then he says "I killed my car man, I killed my car."

I tell him "Yeah bro, but we have to get moving, the cops will be here soon."

Michael says "Let's get Grandpa Larry."

I say "Ok but hurry."

So Michael runs around to the passenger side and pulls the door open.

"Grandpa Larry, we gotta go".

Grandpa Larry says "Just let me sleep here"

"You can't Grandpa Larry, we wrecked the car, the cops are coming, come on, we gotta go." Michael tells him. So Grandpa Larry grabs his sack that he has been selling weed out of, and we take off.

We get about two blocks away and there is a little store with a phone booth in the parking lot. Michael goes into the phone booth just as the cops pulled in.

The police say "Were you guys just in a wreck?" Grandpa Larry is bleeding from his forehead where it hit the dash.

He says "Wreck? No Sir. We were just walking home," in a drunken drawl,

The cop says "Where do you live and do you have some ID?"

At this point the other cop asks me "Were you guys just in a wreck?"

I say "Yes Sir. These two guys picked me up hitchhiking and they were drunk as a skunk. I should never have gotten into the car."

He said "What happened." So I told him "The guy in the phone booth was driving and hotrodding it around a bit and lost control of the car."

He said "Why are you still with them? And do you have any identification?"

"I just wanted to be sure they were alright, and yes sir, here is my ID"

The cop goes and runs my ID and comes back, "Ok Ron, Just wait right here."

Now he is trying to get Michael come out of the phone booth and talk to him. Michael is talking to Doug on the phone, letting Doug know where Michael is stashing the weed he bought from Grandpa Larry and asking Doug to come check the phone booth for his weed because he knows he is going to jail. So Michael is ignoring the cop. Michael finally tells the cop his name is Leonard McGowan and no he doesn't have any ID. Little does he know Leonard has a warrant out for him too.

I tell the cop "Hey officer? It is really cold out here and I only have a tee shirt on, can I go wait inside the store for a while until you to get this all straightened out?"

He says "Sure Ron, but don't go anywhere just yet."

"Ok I won't"

I go into the store and the store clerk is all curious. So I tell him everything. Then I ask him "Is there a back door here?"

He says "Yep. The back door is right through there. I'll tell the cops you went to the bathroom and I haven't seen you since."

I say "Thanks" and I kick rocks. I run and walk and run the 5 miles back home. Then tell my mom everything. She lets me know Doug has been combing the back streets for me. She calls him and lets him know that I made it home safely. Apparently Michael also told Doug I was there and then I wasn't. They figured I was running for cover.

Chapter Seventeen

The next day I get a call for a job in a fish cannery sliming fish, so I take it. When I am there the second day or something, the boss tells me if I know anyone else looking for work to bring them in. I go to my cousin Too Tall Jimmy. He is only 17 but they don't do a lot of checking on those kinds of things back then if you have a SSN you can work for about 3 months. So Too Tall lies about his age and gets hired too. I take him to work with me every day. We party at lunchtime and buy beer on the way home. Life is good.

Well, after we had been working there for about a month. I am taking Too Tall home and he tells me that at the store right by where he lives, the cashier has been taking his money gambling on the pinball machines in the store, but that he had finally won and the cashier wouldn't pay him.

I swing into the store on the way home and the guy is there.

I go in with Too Tall, and I walk up to the cashier he is like 25 years old, clean cut, 6 foot tall and 190 pound real healthy looking.

I politely say, "Hey Dude, you owe Too Tall some money, and he owes me. So I want the money you owe him."

The cashier says "Not my problem"

I tell him "It is now punk, give me my money or I'll kick yer fucken ass"

"That's not how banks do it"

"Do I look like a fucken bank to you, punk? Give me my fucken money before I smash you"

"I don't have it"

"Then take it out of the till or out of the donation jar. You have taken money out of there before so don't act all innocent in front of this other cashier"

"Ok" and pulls the money out of the till. I take the money and go grab a six pack of beer and bring it up to the counter.

He says "Are you 21?"

I am like "Nope"

"I can't sell that to you then"

"But you will sell it to me"

"Ok, but just this time"

"Yep, and every other time I come in here too"

So he rings it up. Then as we are just going out the door he says "And don't come back, Punk".

Well calling someone a Punk is like a killing offence in the joint and I react to it on reflex. I put the beer down and jump over the counter and grab a bunch of his shirt front, bend him backwards over the cash register and say "Don't ever call me punk, mutherfucker or I will kill you"

He squeaks out "But you called me a punk"

"Do you even know what a punk is? A punk is a mutherfucker got his ass took in joint and was made into a girl. Are you going to try to take my ass mutherfucker?"

He squeaks "No'

"Well, I will take your ass punk, if you fucken don't watch your mouth. When do you get off work?"

"I'm not telling you."

Too Tall pipes up "He gets off at 11:00 tonight. Oh and also he has my mini bike at his house."

I tell dude "We want the bike. Where is it?"

"It's at my house, Too Tall knows where."

"Ok, let's go get it."

Dude says "You better not come back here"

"See Ya at 11:00"

"I have a gun."

I tell Too Tall "You hold my shotgun while I stomp a mud hole in his ass and walk it dry ok?"

Too Tall Jimmy grins "Ok"

When we get into the car I give Too Tall his money. Then Too Tall wants to know if we are coming back at 11:00. I tell him probably not. So we go get his mini bike.

When we are dropping the mini bike off at Too Tall's house one of his little buddies, Clint, was there. Now Clint was like the 'Cool Kid' in the neighborhood. Long straight blonde hair, raggedy big bell-bottoms, tie dye tee shirt, you know the type.

We filled Clint in on what we had just done to the store clerk as we drank the beers and Clint says "Let's go back".

I say "Ok". We all pile back into the car and go back to the little store.

We walk in and I go grab a half rack of beer and Clint grabs a bottle of pop.

I get up to the counter and the cashier says "I can't sell you that"

I tell him "Ring it up boy".

"You're going to get me fired"

I say meaningfully "So? Ring it up or I'll kick yer ass, punk!"

He does like he is told, and I walk out laughing. I tell him "Hope yer ready for tonight."

Then the two kids come out and we drive off. We drink the beer and pretty soon it is about 10:30 and the kids want to go wait for the cashier. We go and park about a half block away in a spot where we can watch the front of the store from the comfort of the vehicle like cops on a stake out.

No sooner do we park and a police car pulls into the parking lot of the store. We have a clear view from where we are. The cop comes out of the store gets into his car and the cop backs the car around the side of the store by the garbage cans. Just out of sight to anyone pulling into the parking lot.

So we sit drinking beer and waiting.

The cashier comes out of the store at 11:00.

Now, he is walking back and forth in the parking lot looking up and down the two streets like he is looking for someone. He is swaggering a bit. It is real comical to watch. About 10 minutes later the cop comes out from behind the store. Talks to the cashier then goes back to his car, starts it, pulls out, then drives away.

The cashier then gets into his car and pulls out too. I start my car and pull out and am after the cashier. I pull right behind him turn on my bright lights and he floors it. So the chase is on. We chase him all the way home. He pulls into his driveway, jumps out of his car leaving it running and runs into his house.

We don't even stop. We drive right on by his driveway and go on home laughing and partying the rest of the night.

That cashier will think twice before ripping off some other little kid. I figured he needed to feel what it was like to be on the receiving end of a meaner bully. Not bigger though. He was bigger than I was. But it isn't the size of the dog in the fight, it is the size of the fight in the dog that counts.

Bullies are always afraid of getting hurt so they pick their targets with care. Too Tall was tall but thin as a fence post and Too Tall has a gentle nature.

Chapter Eighteen

I get home and go to bed. My wife is waiting for me. She tells me she wants to get an abortion. I am like no way. She says she doesn't want to raise another kid. That one is enough especially with the life I am leading. I tell her fine if she wants an abortion she can get one, but I am done with her and she has to move out. I won't be with a woman that will kill her unborn children. She says she already made an appointment for in the morning. I tell her "Ok, but if you do make that appointment, don't ever let your shadow darken my door step again. I am keeping the boy. I will take the boy and be gone before you get home" and she will still need another place to come home to, because she won't be welcome here. Pack her shit before she goes. So morning comes, I don't wake her up for her appointment.

When she wakes up she asks "What time is it?" I tell her she has missed her appointment.

She says "It's my body"

I say "Yep and that's my baby in there, I ain't gonna help you kill it" pointing at her belly.

"Are you going to be responsible for it?"

"Yep"

She then relents and says "Ok I'll keep it, but this is the last one"

"Ok"

So no more is said about it, but I knew she wasn't happy about it. Maybe she was right, with the life I was living it was selfish for me to insist she have the kids and I didn't have the right to make her keep the kids. But after it was all said and done I don't have any regrets. I haven't asked her, but if you asked Audrey today I am sure she will have forgiven me my selfishness.

Speaking of Audrey, one night Audrey gets up during the night to go to the bathroom and I wake up enough to realize it is just her. Then I fall back to sleep. Well, when she comes back from the bathroom she tries to be nice and quiet, to not disturb my slumber, but remember I am on warrior status, I am just back from the warzone known as Gladiator School. So as she is sneaking into the room I become aware I am being stalked, but am not fully awake. As soon as she puts a knee on the bed I come alive and have a handful of hair and am slugging her in the head for all I am worth. She screams "Robert! It's me!" and I come awake and stop. I tell her I am so sorry. But the damage is done. I have blacked her eye. I try to get her to wear big sunglasses the next day. Nope, she won't do it. When anyone asks her what happened her pat answer is "He hit me" pointing at me. Then I have to explain what really happened. Man, she was an evil woman.

From then on when she went to the bathroom during the night as pregnant women tend to do, on her way back to bed she would turn the lights on and say "Robert, Sit up" I would say "I'm awake" she would say "No! Sit up!" so I had to sit up before she would turn the lights back off and come to bed.

Well, Betty Jean was dating a guy named Freddy and they were living out in Ashford Washington. Ashford is a nice little out of the way country town.

Audrey and I go out there and do a little partying. Audrey is a real pot head likes to be high all the time. We have a quarter pound. We sell Freddy and Betty an ounce of weed and buy some booze and stay up most of the night with me entertaining folks with card tricks and stacking the deck, dealing poker hands and just for fun setting folks up with full houses and me with four of a kind and telling prison war stories.

In the morning I went outside and looked around. Small town atmosphere, chickens crowing, cows across the street. I can see a couple horses in the distance, right at the base of Mount Rainier. It was beautiful and crisp and clean.

Just the kind of place I wanted to live. (Bad move, folks on escape need to stick to big towns where you can be anonymous and blend in.)

Anyways, there was a place for rent. A one bedroom cabin on an acre of land was 100.00 a month. That's almost too good to be true.

We make plans to move up here on the 1st of August. Just about 3 days from then.

We leave, go back to Seattle to make our plans and gather our belongings.

Well, during that short time, Betty and Freddy get into an argument and she kicked him out. To get back at Betty, Freddy called the police and told them I would be moving into this place within a week's time and of course he told them I had fake ID and what kind of car I was driving. So here I come, right into the trap. Man, I hate small minded people.

We move in on August 2nd 1981, do a little unpacking and about 7:00AM the next morning I have two cop cars and 4 farmer's trucks in my front yard. The Eatonville Police Dept is understaffed so the two police officers have recruited a few of their buddies or family to help.

I see what's in the front yard and run to the back door. Open it up and there are two farmers in flannel shirts with shotguns. Well, that doesn't look good. The place is surrounded.

I walk out front and ask "What Y'all lookin' for?"

One of them farmers jabs his shotgun into the side of my face and says "You, mutherfucker"

"Ok I surrender. My name is Ronald Proteau. What did I do?"

Then one of the police says "Get that shotgun out of his face" then to me "Do you have some ID?"

"Yep sure do. Can I reach into my back pocket?"

The officer says "Go ahead"

So I reach into my pocket real slow eyeing that farmer the whole time and pull out my wallet and ID. I tell him I am Robert's cousin but Robert is not here. I am just helping my cousin's wife get settled in. He looks at my ID and says "Ok." So I think I have it made.

He shows me the warrant with Freddy's name on it as the informer and my photo. But the photo is black and white and like 3 years old. Then as we are reading the warrant it says Robert Thorson has a tattoo of a peacock on his left forearm.

So the cop says "Just to be sure Ron, you don't mind pulling up your sleeve so I can see there is no peacock do you?"

"There is one, Robert and me went into the army together and got the same tattoo on leave."

The cop says "Sorry Ron, I have to take you in to get finger printed. But it won't take more than an hour or so and I'll drive you back out here, but I have to be sure. You can understand that."

I say "Sure bud, no problem" but I know the gig is up. Now this is Pierce County. So they want to transfer me from cop car to cop car at the county lines to get me back to Mason County. Back secure in the prison at Shelton. But Thurston County wants me for 6 months for that ticket I got coming back from the fair on the last escape. Mason

County and DOC (Dept of Corrections) are insistent that I not go to Thurston County and they have first claim and jurisdiction. Thurston claims they have jurisdiction. So WCC (Washington Correction Center) at Shelton sends a pair of armed prison guards to come escort me back to WCC. They have instructions to go around Thurston County with me in custody.

Well, I arrive back at WCC. They do the intake, but there is a question as to who has jurisdiction on me. It appears that Mason County Jail still has legal custody of me. The first thing in the morning, the following day, I am put in a car and delivered back to the County jail. I am not well received there. They put me in the cell that I had locked the guards into a year earlier.

I am thinking, no way. I will be out of here by tonight. I start looking around and I find a piece of metal with a little effort I can break off the window sill. I do and then I sharpen it on the floor. Right after dinner, when the sun is going down, I tell the guard I need a shower. This cell has no shower only a bunk bed and a toilet.

The guard says "Ok, wait about 20 minutes ok?"

"No problem." I am happy and thrilled I can feel the excitement building in my soul. The longer I have to wait the closer it in until nightfall and they will never find me in the dark.

Then 20 minutes or half hour goes by and here comes a guard saying are you ready. I say "Sure am" he has no clue as to what I am ready for. I come out with my towel over my shoulder and start walking in front of the guard as I didn't get a chance to get behind him yet. I walk to the tank door where I expect they will shower me. The guard says "No over here" and we start going toward the sally port.

Then I see them. Two armed prison guards. They say "Thorson drop the towel and cuff up".

"What's up?"

"The Judge signed a court order to keep you in the receiving center while you go to trial. We will be making this trip everyday so get used to it". Then one says "Anything you want to declare before we get back to the receiving center?"

"Yep, how about this?" and I hand them my shank.

The jail guards are all round eyed about that. The prison guards are not even slightly amazed. They inspect it, comment on the poor workmanship and hand it to the jail guard saying "Keep it or dispose of it, we don't want it."

The prison guards then turning to me jokingly say "Damn Thor, can't you stay out of trouble for just one day?"

"Guess not" and we all kind of laugh and they search me, cuff me up and then take me back to the receiving

Chapter Nineteen

So the Kangaroo court begins er... I meant Trial begins. Now my two escape partners have already gone before this Judge and been sentenced to 65 years each. Technically and legally I shouldn't be tried in her courtroom as 1.) She already has prior knowledge of the crime, 2.) She knows the victims on a personal and professional basis. They are guards in her courtroom every single day, and 3.) Judge Carol is feeling a little victimized and vindictive about the whole ordeal.

There have been a total of 23 newspaper articles following the first trial, so any jury pool gathered from the vicinity is going to be tainted and no local attorneys want to defend me on this case because they know they are going to lose.

I ask for a change of venue to say Seattle or somewhere that I might receive a *fairer* trial. Motion denied. That was a big surprise there, huh? They come up with an attorney from somewhere. We get down to brass tacks. I explain to him my defenses and how I am going to try to mess this trial up so I can have a better chance on appeal, because the court of appeals judges won't have a small town stake in this conviction. The state prepares their case and I prepare mine.

Three days before the trial is to begin, I am called into court. The Honorable Carol informs me that my attorney actually works for the District Attorney's office and they have found a defense attorney to take my case, and that this District Attorney will now turn over to my attorney all my pertinent papers and defense strategies.

I am floored. No way can I expect to mount a defense now that I have told the District Attorney all my battle plans. I know there isn't any such animal as a fair trial in America, but isn't there supposed to be fair play rules or something? Don't I have any rights? I know the trial isn't going to be fair but it sure doesn't seem right that they can send a spy from the enemy camp into my war council.

They bring in a lawyer from Olympia and he seems to be a fair guy, but he tells me there is no way he can prepare for trial in 3 days. Then he says but it really doesn't matter as I am not going to win this one. It is a slam dunk with all the cards stacked against me.

My old lawyer (the D.A.) is using things I told him to bring more charges against me. Now, all these new charges they have no proof of, but I am being charged with, the jury is likely to find me guilty of everything anyways. I can't just go with a bench trial as the judge isn't fair and impartial either. So I am up the creek without a paddle.

My new lawyer tried for a continuance and a change of venue. Both are denied by the Honorable Carol. So the trial begins on schedule.

An armed guard it placed between me and the windows and I am kept in leg shackles every day, during the court proceedings.

The D.A. has come to my attorney with a couple plea bargains, even though they know they have me, they would like to spare the county the cost of a full jury trial. But I have nothing to lose.

When I did the escape I figured 10 years for escape. But Mason County broke it down into 4 crimes. First, 2 counts of second degree assault with a deadly weapon on a police officer. Count one the butter knife. Count two the .357, both on Officer Spooner. Then the first degree armed escape and first degree armed robbery for taking the truck at gun point. 10 years for each assault and ten years for the escape and 35 years for the robbery all to be served one after the other for a total for 65 years with all except the Robbery carrying a 7 and a half year mandatory for 22 and a half years minimum. Add that to the robbery I did in Seattle. Then, I still had to go to trial for the escape from WCC that I was brought to this county jail for, when I took over the county jail and did this escape. Well, I didn't have a lot to lose at this point. Can you see where I might not be willing to cooperate?

But there comes a point in all men's lives when they have to cut their losses. Mine came when the little female Guard Janice took the stand. Her testimony went kind of like this.

I quote as best as memory serves "I got down on my knees and prayed to a God I hadn't prayed to since I was 8 years old. Because I just knew they were going to come in and rape me and kill me." The whole time she is on the verge of tears until the last words then she sits there quietly weeping into her hands and shuttering. It was a tragic sight I promise you, and the jury was hanging on every word. The women in the jury were eyeing my with contempt and the men looked like they would just as soon forgo the trial and hang me from the flag pole out front.

I turn to my lawyer at this point and say "Tell the DA if they drop the weapon on the original charges and drop all the new charges, I'll cop to the original charges. Because if they drop the weapon all of the mandatory's go away and the Board of Prison Terms and Paroles don't have to give me more than a couple years on each sentence.

He goes to the D.A. with my offer and they take it. They draw up a plea agreement that says I am pleading guilty to all the crimes with to-wit a deadly weapon and firearm. I object of course, so they draw a line through the *deadly weapon* part but not the firearm part. But I didn't notice or thought that it wouldn't matter. So like a dumbass I sign it. This was effectively Ineffective assistance of counsel. I was screwed by the system again. Back in those days deadly weapon or firearm carries the same mandatory. So why would I object to the wording if I wasn't objecting to the sentence? But they must have had it planned that way.

If my lawyer was on my side, and he is supposed to know the law, why didn't he tell or warn me? Unless of course, my Lawyer who was suppose to be looking out for my best interest, was supposed to be defending his client with vigor according to the oath he took, must have been in the conspiracy too.

Truth, Justice and the American Way? Where the hell is Superman when you need him? Well, there just isn't any Superman and there isn't much truth, justice or honor in 'The American Way' anymore.

We proceed to sentencing and the Honorable Carol has to have the last say of course.

She says "No one has escaped from my county jail in 16 years." Pausing for effect I cut in "Well I did!"

She turned beet red and said "And for that reason Mr. Thorson, I will set an example for anyone else considering following your footsteps. I am sentencing you on count one to 10 years for the crime of Assault in the second degree and setting a 7 and a half year mandatory. On count two, escape in the first degree, I am sentencing you to 10 years and setting a 7 and a half year mandatory. On count three, Assault in the second degree I am sentencing you to 10 years and a 7 and a half year mandatory and on count four, Robbery in the first degree I am setting your maximum at 35 years. I further more am setting these terms to run consecutive to each other and consecutive to any prior sentence you may be serving, as well as recommending to the Board of Prison Terms and Paroles that you don't be released for 60 years."

I say "Cool, can I go now?"

So the cut and dried version is I got 22 and a half years in mandatories as a minimum sentence unless the Parole Board sets a longer minimum. I could get out in about 17 years for good behavior or goodtime if I keep my nose clean and the Parole Board is generous. Not likely to happen in my case. The guards respect me and maybe even like what I do as far as stopping the ducks from being abused. But that doesn't wash with the Parole Board because all they see is that I have a whole lot of infractions for fighting and a lot of my *victims* are going to the hospital. They don't know the reason behind the fights nor do they care. The guards must infract me for fighting too, even though they know why I fight. So I get tossed under the bus so to speak, but it has to be that way, my life depends on it.

Since W.S.R. is my parent institution they ship me back there. The transfer to Walla Walla is forgotten. Remember that's what started all this. I didn't want to go to Finishing School. So once again, I have gotten my way. Man, the lengths a guy has to go to, to get his own way sometimes.

Well, I get back to Gladiator School and of course everyone is glad to see me. My Trainer Michael says "Man, Thor, glad you're back, this place is just plain boring without you here."

I say "Thanks a lot buddy, but I wasn't missing you that much." They get me a care package with coffee, cigarettes and the basics, soap, shampoo etc. Life goes back to normal as much as life can ever be normal in Gladiator School.

My new wife is coming up to see me every week and bringing my son. She is like 8 months pregnant. Then after a month she is bringing up my daughter Angela, too. Audrey is down to like 120 pounds after the baby is born. She has never been that thin before.

I go to the Parole Board during this time. They are not pleased with me to say the least. They set my minimum term to a date they will all be retired by. They give me 380 months. 31 years 6 months. That is so much time that a person's mind can't quite grasp it. Your mind just doesn't wrap around it and it all seems kind of unreal. So your mind only records it as a set of numbers nothing more.

I go to a visit and Audrey asks "What happened at the Parole Board meeting?" so I tell her I got 380 months. She says "That's not too bad, what is that like 3 years?"

"No babe that's like 31 years and some change."

She just says "Oh"

She goes home and I never see her or my kids again. She won't accept my phone calls or anything. So now I do what I must do. I write her 15 to 20 page love letters everyday because I love her with all my heart and soul. My young mind can't accept that she would leave me because of this. I just don't have the wisdom yet. Wisdom is gained in the fires of disappointment and pain, unlike knowledge that is gained from books and schools.

But in the mean while, as I wait for my wife to come back to me, I start looking for a girlfriend to send me clothing and food packages and a little money for my books. Little fat welfare moms are the best for this. Everybody has one and they all have friends so finding a replacement isn't too hard. Little young fat welfare moms with kids in tow fill the visiting rooms of prisons across the USA. They are the mainstay for lonely felons. I take my cellies (cell partner) ex ole lady. Annette has a job and a young son named Danny. She is bigger than most, about 300 pounds, but she has more money than most and a generous heart. She is not pretty but I don't really care. She is willing to visit and buy me things, so I am good with it. As it turns out she will be my meal ticket for the next 20 years off and on.

Chapter Twenty

Around 1983 the administration is trying to gain control of the prison. They have found that if they try to take to many privileges away from the felons, all at once, we will riot. So they have taken all the leaders of the clubs and shipped them out of state. Then who ever took their place and shipped them out of state, too. So now we get a bus load of felons from Walla Walla. One of them is a lifer and runs for the Pres of the Lifers, a spot which was just opened up. We are ecstatic; a Walla Walla felon is going to be Pres. So we vote Terry in as our new President. He has a punk named Buddy with him from Walla Walla. We jokingly called them the Pres and the first Lady.

Well, pretty quick I am noticing that the Pres. is saying the administration is going to be taking this or that and we are going to let them have this one thing, then that one thing and so it keeps going until we don't have much of our freedoms left.

Now, we have been having dances every other Sunday since I can remember and on the picnic tables where felons sat with their girlfriends or wives sheets were used for table clothes. Well, the felons and their ladies have been going under these tables for a quickie since the beginning. First it is the table clothes that go, then the dances are discontinued and our Pres. is ok with all that. The Lifer's Club sets the tone for the whole prison. Every other club kind of waits to see how the Lifers will react to any given situation and then they react accordingly, so if we accept it, so do they usually.

Next, our Lifer's Club meetings start beginning with the Pres. Saying "Everyone bow your head for a moment of silent prayer".

Well, I, for one, am not feeling the need for any prayer, forgiveness or redemption. I stand up and say "Whoa, what the hell is going on here? I thought this was a Lifers Meeting. Not some Jesus-Freak convention. I must be in the wrong place. See ya." When I walk out, about ten Lifers must feel where I am coming from, because they get up and walk out too. That was about a third of the Lifers Club back then.

Later that day, I am out walking in the big yard and Buddy, 'The First lady', comes up to me and says "You better watch what you say in the Lifers Meetings."

I say "Or what? What is anyone going to do if I don't?" The new Sergeant of Arms is with her, but he is just some scared pencil neck kid that I would smash in a heartbeat. He knows it too, so he isn't saying anything.

I look at him and say "What you going to do, mutherfucker?"

"Nothing"

"I thought not."

The First Lady flounced and says "Well you're kicked out of the Lifers Club then." I laughed right out loud. I couldn't help myself that was such an off the wall stupid statement.

I said "You stupid fucken punk, weren't you there when I walked out? Who would want to be a part of that fucken weak ass club anymore, anyway?"

Shortly afterwards, we found out Terry and the first lady were shipped here from Walla Walla, right out of Protective Custody. The Lifers Club never fully recovered from that. They should have killed Terry and Buddy right then. Then, maybe, they could have recovered, but no one did. The Lifers club became a joke. The leaders were puppets for the administration.

PRISON STORIES FROM GLADIATOR SCHOOL

It finally died a slow death ending around 1995. The administration has done the same or similar things to all the clubs. Trying to get their own men in the clubs in positions of power, and it had worked. The prisoners clubs have ceased to be an opposing force; they have ceased to resist the administration's will.

The days of the true convicts and Guards were numbered and the dawn of the *Inmate and Correctional Officer* had begun. The guards would no longer tell the Lifers Club when Sex Offenders came to our prison, nor would they turn a blind eye to our killing them. We used to get 30 days in the hole for getting caught killing a Rape-o, because we weren't suppose to get caught; we were supposed to be smarter than that. Now, they are taking you downtown and charging you with murder one and giving life without parole for ridding society of that scum and the scum are getting civilly committed called criminally insane and collecting a welfare check for like 800 a month and have no bills to pay. You're paying for this with your tax dollars.

1983 was the first time I can remember anyone being charged with murder for killing another Convict.

Bowman was a boxer and a Skin (Indian/Native American). He had just a couple months left on his life term. He had done 13 years. He was a dangerous felon with an attitude. Well, there were these two other felons, one a lifer, the other just doing a five year bit for auto theft, that were selling marijuana. They had sold Bowman a Dime (10 dollars worth of marijuana). When Friday comes, Snowman and John go up to Bowman and say "Hey bro, where is your money? "

Bowman playing the hard ass felon says "What money? I don't owe you shit," and pops John in the face. John goes down and Bowman walks away. John is just a young kid 19 or 20 years old and has no real skill at fighting. Now, technically, since Bowman fought for it and won he didn't owe Snowman and John anything. But a technicality doesn't always get you off the hook in the joint.

That night, during the evening meal, John and the Snowman walk up behind Bowman as he is eating his dinner and both ram shanks deep into his back, kidney high. Bowman stands up turns around and falls dead. Now, those kids HAD TO DO THAT! If they had not done it they would have been robbed by everyone and had they been lesser men, might have been turned into punks or ran into P.C. If they had been tried by a Jury of their Peers… well their peers are convicts, obviously. So they were tried by a jury of people who did not understand the laws of our society. What they did was self-defense. For them it wasn't just 10 dollars worth of pot, it was their life or his. They are warriors so they valued their lives over his. So, he had to die. It wasn't personal and Bowman should have been watching his ass a little closer. But he had been on top so long he didn't think anyone would or could touch him. Well, that's a mistake he will never make again. Even the Indians understood that Bowman had brought it on himself and didn't react to it. But why they didn't warn him when two white boys came walking amongst them toward Bowman's back, I don't know. Maybe they just thought the kids were going to fight Bowman and wanted to watch. But they were equally responsible for his death. Had not the Snowman and John killed Bowman they could have never did business in the joint again because no one would have paid them if they didn't respect them as men.

That was the last killing inside for almost a decade because both the Snowman and John were charged downtown and given life sentences to run consecutive to their current sentences.

So now, rats and rape-os could walk the big yard and only get beat up everyday. They wouldn't die and that also means that rapists would be getting out of prison in the future. Society wasn't as happy about that as they thought they would be. You can tell by the lock them up forever laws that were passed in 1995. Now, when society is paying all the medical, dental and health care bills for all these senior felons that are no longer a danger to society, and all the taxes keep going up as we build more prisons to hold all these old felons. Well, we will see. Washington already has a geriatrics prison for old felons in wheel chairs, who is paying for that? Oh you are! Those old men are no longer a danger to anyone. But you will pay for their medical and burial before long. From the looks of it, the prison system isn't working and it is going to continue to cost the tax payers a lot of money to house felons too old to commit crimes anymore, as well as sex offenders that would be dead if society hadn't of rained on our parade.

It was right about this time that the prisons were taken away from DSHS (Department of Social Health Services) and DOC (Department of Corrections) was created to take over the handling of the Prison Systems.

As one of their first official acts, they created Women Guards. Now, putting sissy guards in a man's prison is one thing but some dumbass decided that women should have an equal opportunity to be abused, and what women… Man, they were all good looking and came to work in these uniforms that looked like they were painted on. I was living on Baker side at this time in Baker 2-1 (Second Tier-First Cell.) In those days, a lot of the time the guards were lax and didn't see to it that your cell door was locked in between movement periods. So mine was often left ajar.

Well, on Baker side a little 125 pound Blond Farrah Fawcett looking chick about 5'2" is stationed, all by her-self. Her name was Correctional Officer Swanburg.

Sitting in my cell, I hear some taunting going on. My door is unlocked. Then I hear some guys calling her filthy names and it is escalating. Pretty quick something bad is going to happen, I can tell. I step out of my cell and see like 6 guys down around the guards station. Behind the desk looking pretty frightened is little blonde Swanburg.

I step out of my cell and I say "That's enough, leave her alone." I didn't raise my voice, I just said it calmly, but it was enough.

The felons look at me like they can't believe I just said that, so one of the braver ones says tauntingly "What, Thor, you protecting guards now?"

I reply calmly but pinning the spokesperson with my eyes menacingly "Nope, but I will protect a women in need of protecting, and although she wears a guard's uniform, she is still a woman underneath, so step off and give her 30 feet."

The felons grumble and probably talk bad about me under their breath but they move away. So I go back into my cell.

A few minutes later CO Swanburg came up and sat on the rail in front of my cell and wanted to talk. I told her "Look, lady, you're a guard, we can't be friends and you can't hang out in front of my cell, you will put my life in danger."

So she left. But the next day there was a bunch of grapes on my bed when I got home from work and the next day some homemade cookies. Every day, for a long time, I had something good on my bed after work and I wasn't one to complain.

Later that day or maybe it was the next day. I was confronted by some Lifers and solid convicts. They wanted to know what the deal was with CO Swanburg, and me protecting her.

They said women don't belong here and they didn't want women pat searching them.

I said "I don't know about you, but I would much rather have a woman running her hands all over my body then one of these fag male guards. But you know, each to their own, I guess, and I like looking at women. So I don't have a problem with them and I am not going to let some dickweeds abuse women in front of me, guard uniform or not."

I knew I had them when I said the thing about women running their hands all over our bodies. So that was the end of it.

Chapter Twenty One

One day Spike, Dusty and I are playing handball and smoking pot. It is a beautiful July 4th. The prison has served hotdogs and pop in the big yard. The riot hasn't started yet, so we three are lying in the grass out in front of the Gym and Spike has played against Dusty and I and beat us single handed at handball. Spike says to Dusty "Dusty, ten years from now, I am going to ask you, I'll Say 'Dusty, where were you on July 4th 1985.' And you'll say 'Why Spike I was in Monroe with you, lying in the grass and it was a fine sun shining day. We were smoking pot enjoying the afternoon after you spanked Thor and Me single handily at a game of handball.'" We all laughed. Spike was just a funny guy and I know we were in prison, but even there a person can have fun if he allows himself to.

Well the riot didn't happen until about 6:00pm that day and wasn't anything to write home about. Don't really remember too much about it. It was just one of many and the memories all blur and run together after a while.

After the riot the prison decides to do a little remodeling and put in bigger front doors. Now they do fence this area off with barbed wire and cyclone fencing and for most felons that would have been enough, but I ain't most felons. I want out and am always looking for flaws in the security. By October 3rd I have seen the way out. Now, at this time, I am celled up with the Yard Monster. He is just a naturally big corn-fed boy. There is one in every joint, 6 foot something and 240 or more pounds of solid natural muscle, never worked out just naturally big and strong. But he got much bigger when he hit the weight pile in Walla Walla. I tell him about my plan and he is game, we leave tonight at the 8:30 gate movement. It will be getting dark. It is the last movement of the day.

The construction workers have dug trenches with a back hoe and they lead up to the hole in the wall that just has an eight foot cyclone fence across it and a single strand of barbed wire. The hole is 12 feet high. Yes it is right under a tower manned with an armed guard, but my logic says he won't be looking straight down, he will be watching the yard and none of the towers can see where we will jump the fence. Only passing felons will see us, where we are going over the fence. So we should be ok on that score.

So the Yard Monster, (Dave) and I make our move. What we didn't count on was that there was an inmate in our midst that was a cop in Idaho before being convicted for dealing drugs and sent to our prison. Coker, well he saw us go over the fence and immediately went into the kitchen where a guard is posted watching the felons playing games and drinking coffee. Then Coker said to the whole room, guards included, "There are some guys escaping out by the crane".

Well, I want to let you know that put a crimp in my style, about 6 guards ran out with shotguns and stood in front of the opening.

Can't go back and can't go forward. We are caught between a rock and a hard spot, so we go to the hole. Well, that's a big surprise there, huh?

Now, I never was one to lie about what I had done. Convicts do deny a lot of things, but with write ups ... well, we look at it this way, it is our job to try to get around the rules and it's the guard's job to catch us. But if they do catch us so what? What are they going to do? Put us in a cell? We already live in a cell. Threaten to take goodtime? The parole board is the only one that can take goodtime and they almost never do. So if we admit to it when we are guilty, then when we go in and deny we did it, our word carries more weight. So at the hearing when they ask, "How do you plead?" I say "Guilty". 10 days in the hole and transfer to Walla Walla.

Well, this time there is no getting around it, all the holes are plugged and I am going to Finishing School.

I get there and they separate the Yard Monster and me, putting the Yard Monster in 6 Wing and me in 8 Wing.

I am put into a bikers four man cell. No big deal, I get along with bikers. No one is home when I get there. I take out all my paperwork and lay it on my bed, so it is easy to see and read. Then I go to yard. That way no one has to ask who I am or what I am in for. They can see it when they come in.

Second day I am there this big muscle bound Mexican named Poncho stops by in front of my cell and looks in at me.

He asks me "You just get here?"

I say "Yeah."

"You got money on your books?"

Now I am thinking he has something he wants to sell, so I say "Yeah."

He takes me by surprise when he says "Ok, then you are going to order me some store!"

I say "Ok."

Then he leaves. My biker type, hard convict cellies, who had been listening to all my war stories last night, are all looking at me out of the corner of their eyes like this can't be real. Because our main source of entertainment is our life stories and our crime stories.

So one says to me "Dude, what was that?" what he meant was you're not going to punk out and take that are you? But he didn't say that.

So I say "The door was closed, what did you expect me to do? Wait until he isn't so well protected and then see what happens"

I can see my cellies are beginning to wonder a little bit about me. Am I who and what I say I am or am I just talking shit trying to make myself look tougher then I am? They are willing to wait and watch, but if I puss out, they will keep all my property.

Next day at lunch, Poncho walks up to me with his head down and his hands behind his back and says smugly, "You ordered my store right?"

I say "Sure" and uppercutted him to the chin, then through a right cross that landed solidly. Poncho went down and did the funky chicken on the floor, flopping around with his eyes rolling up in his head. I thought 'Oh Shit, I killed the dumb motherfucker,' but he came too and jumped up to his feet. Put up his dukes and I stepped in threw a solid left jab and a right cross and down he went again flopping all over the floor like a fish. The riot windows above the serving lines opened and three guards with bean bag guns popped their heads out to cover the crowd, someone through a glass salt shaker at the armed guards.

Then the search and escort guards at the door ran over and grabbed me. Poncho got up and threw a haymaker that glanced off my shoulder and hit my cheek. I told him "Go ahead take another one, because you can't hit me if no one is holding me."

The guards then grabbed Poncho too. They took Poncho to the hospital and me to the hole. After a 24 hour observation period, Poncho was also brought down to the hole, but put on a different tier.

I get infracted for assault and Poncho gets infracted for fighting. I ask why am I get an assault beef which is a more serious infraction and Poncho only getting a fighting beef. I am told that the administration has decided that I know martial arts.

I say "I have no formal training".

They say "You have Special Forces military training".

I tell them "No, I don't"

They say "Don't deny it. It's in your central file".

So I say "Ok."

So from this point on I am no longer infracted for fighting. There is no self defense clause in prison. If you defend yourself you were fighting. If you roll up in a ball on the ground and don't defend yourself, you were fighting. Only now your run the risk of other felons taking everything you own and maybe fucking you in the butt to boot. Now to answer that question nagging in the back of your mind, no I do not have Special Forces training I been in prison since I was 17 years old remember. But a lot of my cellies were Special Forces and they did teach a little here and there.

There is no write up for horse playing either. As Sergeant Bowman so eloquently puts it "You were either fucking or fighting which was it?" They won't let you say you were horse playing because that might be a cover up for something more serious, you don't want to admit to. Since they believe I have training, I get assault beefs instead of fighting write ups from this point on.

Poncho and I both do 10 days in the hole. The punishment is the same. We both get out and go back to 8 Wing. I am put into another cell with three different bikers. They have heard the story and saw it unfold, so there is no problem even though my paperwork is still in the property room and I don't have it yet to show them.

Poncho sees me in the dining hall and tells me "Now, you owe me double". Well, he never set an amount that I had to buy in the first place. So what is double of the ass whipping I gave him? This shows why he is in prison. He is not a very smart person.

On the way back to my cell, there is a blind spot where the guards can't see in 8 Wing. It is about 10 feet by 12 feet with a cyclone fence on one side and walls on the other. As I am coming up to it, I see Poncho peeking around the corner. I am walking with a biker that stands 6'4" and looks like a body builder. Maybe he already knows what is up ahead, but if he does, he didn't warn me. That might be why he is walking with me, I don't know, but I do warn him, "When we go around the corner up ahead I am going into a fight. If it is one on one, I am good, but if there is more than one I may need a hand."

He says "I got your back Bro." That felt real good in my heart right about then. Because I didn't know how many I was up against.

I walk around the corner and all I see is a wall of maybe 30 Mexicans with Poncho standing in front of them, a little scary, but you can't run in the joint, there is no place to go. All you can do is fight and die well.

I step through the door into the massacre. I see movement behind me and spin.

There behind me, that I couldn't see because they were leaning against the wall on either side of the door were about 30 bikers. My heart swells with pride. As they close off my retreat, not that I had any intentions of retreating anyways. I was prepared to sell my life dearly and maybe this proud biker walking with me would lose his life too. But now with all these solid warriors at my back, I know the arena is mine.

Poncho wants to talk some shit first, to grand stand, to try to build his courage or scare me, I don't know which, but I see no reason for talk. I step right in and start jabbing and hooking, Poncho falls back against the cyclone fence and I proceed to pound on him, hooking from both directions. He is just trying to cover up and get away from me. Then he reaches out and grabs a hold of me around the waist. Now he is clinging to me for dear life, bleeding from his nose and mouth and I split his cheek open. He is bleeding all over my white tee shirt and has yet to swing back. I elbow smash him on the back just below his neck as he clings to me and he goes down to one knee then comes up and runs through the wall of Mexicans, they part for him like the red sea and close behind him so I can't give chase.

From the other side of the Mexicans, Poncho yells "We ain't done yet, Punk"

So I yell back to Poncho, "Well then, come on back I ain't tired and I wasn't done yet either".

Well, I lived on that first tier where the fight occurred. So I rushed to my cell and took the bloody tee shirt off and flushed it down the toilet and put on a fresh tee shirt. Yes, Prison toilets will take a tee-shirt without a stitch. Then we waited because Poncho had to go passed the guards to get to his cell on the second tier and he was soaked in blood and bleeding badly. We were all happy and thrilled that the fight had gone so well. Ponchos inability to fight had made me look like I was even a better fighter then I was. My biker cellies were impressed. My reputation grew.

Pretty soon the goon squad rolled up in front of the cage and said "Thorson, step out and cuff up." I reckon it didn't take a rocket scientist to figure out what had happened.

Back to the hole I go. Now, in the hole, if you put an empty toilet paper roll over the drain in the sink and blow real quick and hard all the water in the water trap will go down the drain. Then since all the drains go to the same pipe, if you talk down your drain it will carry to any other cell that has the water blown out of the drain. This is our prison cell phone system.

I heard Poncho talking to someone saying, "Get that long haired guy, he is a rat." Poncho is trying to get someone else to do what he couldn't do. So next day, I come out to yard on the tier and this big black guy named Armstrong says "Poncho talking about you?"

Well, you have to know by now I am not one to do a lot of talking when there is fighting to do. So I kick ole Armstrong in the knee and start throwing down on him, but Armstrong is a boxer and a good one. It isn't a cake walk. I am getting as good or more then I am giving. Had it gone on much longer I might have lost this one.

The guards charge in and grab Armstrong, twist his arms behind his back and bend him over. I kick him in the mouth and stand him back up, knocking a couple of his teeth out. The guards rushed me and shoved me back into my cell, locking the door. They then escort Armstrong to the hospital.

One of the guards, Correctional Officer Pease, came back to my cell and starts talking shit to me. Saying how he could bend me over and fuck me. I tell him "Only thing holding you back is fear and commonsense and we know you don't have any commonsense." He looks like he might be considering coming into my cell by himself. Guess he liked Armstrong or something. I tell him "Don't do it, don't let 30 seconds of stupidity fuck off the rest of your life."

Then he did. He said "Fuck you, Thorson, you ain't nothing but a Punk," now those are killing words in the joint. Up to this point it was all fun and games. Talking shit and bantering is how we pass time in the joint but there are lines that no one can cross. CO Pease knew he was taking it to another level, but being a dumbass, he didn't know who I was and hadn't read my jacket yet, so he didn't care. Pease had crossed the line of no return. He had made a dangerous enemy and risked his life over losing a banter session. What a dumbass. Maybe he thought, being a guard, I wouldn't or couldn't touch him. Well, that kind of thinking can and will get you killed.

I told him, "You can't walk Population any more, Punk." My saying 'punk' to him was me putting him on notice we were playing for keeps now.

He said "I will be walking it today".

I said "That's because I ain't out there, I get out of the hole, Punk, and you don't survive one shift. Count on it". I meant every word of it. Even though CO Pease was dumb enough to let his mouth pass checks his ass couldn't catch and think he could handle it, his superiors knew we could not be on the same mainline again. That guard uniform was not bullet proof and wouldn't stop a shank either. They knew I didn't threaten. CO Pease would get hurt or die. I don't make empty threats and they knew it after reading my jacket. I made prophecies. They had to find a way to defuse the situation. The easiest way was to get rid of me.

Finishing School didn't want me anymore.

Chapter Twenty Two

So they sent me out to the Super Max they had just built. I.M.U. (Intensive Management Unit) is what they called it. It was for long term isolation. This is where the most dangerous felons are kept. You are in your cell 23 hours out of every day. You go to yard all by yourself and usually at 4:30 in the morning. The florescent lights stay on 24 hours a day. The air conditioner is on 24 hours a day, summer and winter, creating white noise. The walls are all white. Sheets, blankets and coveralls are all white. Tee shirts, socks and underwear are all white.

It was all reminiscent of 1953 Korean Prisoner of War camp torture tactics. Where they try to break down the Korean prisoners mentally and make them turn on their own people. It was psychological warfare that we tried back then. Brain washing is what it is called. Now, the Washington State Prison system was trying it on the prisoners.

There was one named Big Al, he was a Con Boss. He found the proofs and so started a class action lawsuit, which we won, but not for a few years. They mentally tortured felons for about 6 years before the High Courts of our Corrupt Nation saw fit to give us relief. To appease the High Courts, The Institution dyed all the sheets, blankets, socks, tee shirts, towels, etc., pink. Since the high courts had not said what color we had to have, only that the state prison system could not keep us in all white, the Washington state prison system decided pink would be a good color. They also put mirrors in the shower areas. As prior to that, there were no mirrors. It was all a part of trying to cause us to lose our identity by not being able to see ourselves.

Some guys found the pink color degrading and the guards used it when harassing us. Saying things like "Oh, you look real tough in those pink panties". Or other such references. Me, I didn't care. I am mono-chromatic color blind. I only see black and white anyways, so to me it is just a light shade of gray. I like the color pink personally, but a lot of hard felons refused to wear the pink underwear, so they just didn't wear underwear. Now when they take you to the shower in cuffs all you can wear is your underwear and socks. So if you're not wearing underwear you go in just your socks.

Now, while I was in IMU, I was relatively quiet, I worked out all day, doing about 800 pushups a day as well as jumping jacks and tricep extensions off the sink and my Katas. This kept me warm since it was winter and the air conditioner was on.

When you are stuck in an eight by ten room with no books, no TV and no radio, you must find a way to entertain yourself. I worked out. Not bothering anyone. I also was not getting any mail although I was writing a lot.

Now, for some unknown reason this short little pencil neck guard named Black decided it was his job to mess with me.

So every week I would order my 3 books from the library and when they came, CO Black would show them to me then say "Oh you're refusing to take the books? Ok I'll send them back." And mark down I had refused them and send them back. He was keeping my mail and putting it in a plastic garbage bag. I didn't know this about my mail, but I did about the books. He would come into my cell every time I went out for a shower or yard and take my Chess pieces I made out of toilet paper and he would break the lead on my pencils.

They always gave us tooth powder instead of toothpaste. It was good stuff, whitened your teeth better than anything I ever saw. Just like comet.

Well, I devised a little trap. Just a prank if you will, for CO Black. The tooth powder came in a little manila envelope about 2 inches wide and 4 inches tall. I carefully tore one apart and saved the lick and stick part from 3 other envelopes. I piled all the tooth powder on top of the one envelope I had opened and licked the sticky part and stuck it to the ceiling right above the door. Then took the other three sticky parts and used them to stick the other three sides up to the ceiling. So I had about two tablespoons of toothpowder resting loosely on top of this paper stuck to the ceiling. Now, CO Black was like 5'5" and 130 pounds. CO Black was just a little guy with a short man complex, so for three days I watch him search my cell and not find it.

So on the fourth day, on the way to the shower after he had cuffed me up but before the door opens, I look at him, take a quick glance at the ceiling above the door, then back at him and turn around, so I can back out of the cell as the door is opened.

I step out and CO Black, true to course, steps in to see what he can steal from me. He walks half way into the cell and stops dead. Turns around looks at me, and then looks at the ceiling where I had looked. A great big shit eating grin comes over his face and he takes one step and jumps up and grabs the paper.

The tooth powder hits him in the forehead and poofs over the rest of his face. The other guard and I are cracking up laughing at CO Black. The other guard, when he gets his laughter under control, says "Good one, Thor."

CO Black is not seeing the humor but says "Alright, you got me this time". He can't write me up for it even if he could think up a rule I was breaking, because it would make him look like a fool in the hearing and all the other guards would be laughing at him, too. But he wasn't happy that I had gotten the best of him.

Up to this point, everything I had done back was just in play, making a game out of it. I would put anything I wanted to keep like my coffee packs in my underwear and take it back and forth to the shower with me.

Well, I put up with this treatment for a couple months and never let on I knew he was singling me out. Nor do I know why he was singling me out, maybe CO Pease was his friend. Now, going to the shower or yard, you had to be cuffed up (hand cuffed) before they let you out of the cell. They would open the food slot in the cell door, and then you would have to put your hands behind your back and through the tray slot so they could cuff you. The Correctional Officers (not *Guards*, these guys wouldn't make a pimple on a real guard's ass, they had no respect coming from me) would then put the hand cuffs on you and escort you to the shower or yard.

Well, coming back from a shower in December 1986, CO Black was escorting me back to my cell while his co-worker went up stairs to get another inmate on the floor above out of the shower. CO Black took this opportunity to practice some sadistic pressure point tactics on my arm.

I stopped dead in my tracks and brought my heel up like you would kick yourself in the butt, only into CO Black's nuts. Then I pulled free of his grip and kicked him solidly in the nuts again, he doubled over then I kicked him in the head and he flipped over onto his back. I started kicking him in the head and stomping on his head. He is screaming to his partner to come downstairs and help him, but the other CO has to lock up the felon he was escorting first.

He comes downstairs and sees CO Black curled up in a ball and me stomping a mud hole in his ass and says "Thorson, Lock up!"

I say "You want some of this too?"

"No, will you please just lock up?"

"Sure."

I kick CO Black one last time in the head and walk into my cell. The door closes behind me, so I sit down and put my legs through my cuffs so my hands are in front of me.

CO Black is at the cuff port and yells angrily, "Thorson, uncuff!"

Well, I know if I put my hands through the port he will jerk them hard and possible injury me badly. He is not a happy camper and is a vindictive sadistic little piece of shit.

So I say "No way, CO Black, why don't you come and get them!"

CO Black Repeats his demand and so do I.

CO Black calls the Goon Squad. I put my bar of soap in my sock and tie a knot in the end of the sock by the toe so the stitching won't give if I hit someone. I throw a cup of water and some shampoo on the floor by the door so the goons will have a slippery time of it. Black is leading this show and you can see the sadistic thrill in his eyes.

But oop's, just then a lieutenant comes in and says "What's going on here?" CO Black says "This convict attacked me and now won't uncuff."

The LT. comes to my door and says "Thorson, why won't you uncuff?"

I tell the LT. "I don't trust CO Black, he is an asshole. But if you will take the cuffs off, you can have them"

"Really, no tricks?"

"Word of Honor"

The LT. turns to Black and says "Give me the keys" CO Black is totally disappointed as he sees his prey escape, but gives up the keys.

I ask the LT. "Do you want me to put the cuffs back behind my back first?"

He says "That won't be necessary," then he removes my cuffs and tells the Goon Squad "You can stand down, the crisis has been averted."

CO Black comes back in about a half hour with about 4 of his buddies. He demands, "Thorson, cuff up!" I grab my sock with the bar of soap in it and start swinging it over my shoulder like numchucks.

"Come on in," I reply.

He repeats his demand and I reply, "The first one through the door is going home in a pine box and the next one is leaving in an ambulance, so come on in. Let the party begin!"

CO Black says if they have to come in by force I will get hurt. I just keep taunting them, "You got the easy part done punk, the talking part. Now do it, quit talking about it and do it. What, you scared? Only thing holding you back is fear and commonsense and we know you don't have any commonsense fucking with me. Come on in, you have me outnumber five to one, come on in, but you can only come through the door one at a time, mutherfucker, and I'll smash you, one at a time"

They got tired of the game because they didn't have the authority to come in and the LT wasn't going to back them on this and they knew I would hurt one or more of them before they got me. It wouldn't be worth it, so they left. But from that point on I never went to yard or shower when CO Black was on duty.

On Christmas Eve, a guy comes to my cell and says "Robert Thorson?"

I say "Yes"

He says "This is for you" and hands me divorce papers from my darling wife. She is divorcing me when I am at my absolute lowest. I am feeling deserted by all my family and friends, no one is writing me and I am under constant attack from my captures. She couldn't have picked a more devastating moment to back stab me in the back if she had tried.

Christmas came and went. I still haven't received any mail from anyone. So I have written all my people off. Told them if they didn't have the time to drop me a line, I didn't need them either. They could all fuck off and die for all I cared.

New Years rolls around and CO Black takes a ten day vacation. His partner brings my mail. Like 4 or 5 months worth or more of mail, Christmas cards, birthday cards and more than 200 letters. He doesn't tell me that CO Black has been holding my mail, but it is understood. Just like CO Black has been sending my library books back, saying I rejected them. For a year, while I am out in IMU, I never get a book from the library. All I can get is a bible from the Preacher. I read the Bible cover to cover 6 times. Still don't believe any of the crap. No salvation for me I guess.

Well, I have been in IMU for about a year now. CO Black is still trying to mess with my head, but I am getting my mail anyways. I eat, sleep and work out all day.

About this time I guess, my mind starts to snap. I start thinking about killing people for the first time. Not killing them quick and easy. Not killing in self defense but killing for pleasure. I want to go shoot or run over a guard. Any guard, it doesn't matter to me as long as they are dead. Then I want to go to his or her funeral, dressed all in black leather on a black motorcycle with a small black automatic weapon, and opening up on the crowd about chest high. Because I know a lot of other guards will be there and I stand a good chance of killing a few more. If I don't kill them, I figure chest high will at least catch their women and children in the head. That would be better then killing them, because then they will be suffering some of the pain I am going through, and on a motorcycle I can make a quick get away without being recognized. I lay awake at night, plotting the demise of my enemies.

IMU is having an effect on me, but I don't think it is the effect that my captors are hoping for. It is not making me think I should be good. It is turning me into a mad dog, more than one guard is afraid of me at this point. I am pretty much healed, after a fashion, now I think no thanks to the penal system. I had to work through it myself. Had I escaped at this time…..? Well let's just say it was a good thing I didn't.

One day, CO Black is serving lunches. As he gets ready to put my lunch down in my tray slot, he spits in my tray. I take the apple that was being served that day and throw it out the tray slot and hit ole CO Black in the back of the head with it. Then when CO Black come back to grab my tray I side kick it into him, covering him in the food and his own spit. That pisses him off and he goes into a rage.

That night at dinner, they bring me something that looks like the fritters from 20 years before. Only now they are calling it Nutra loaf. I tell them I am not eating it. They say "Well you're on it for 10 days for throwing your lunch on CO Black." Well, I had done 10 day fasts before, back in the days of fritters, so every day I refuse this shit they are passing off as food. (Socrates Said "You can judge the civilization of a society by looking within its prisons walls.) We are supposed to be a civilized country? How do we treat each other like this?

Ten days came and went. They were still bringing the Nutra loaf to me. I complained. CO Black said "You're on Nutra loaf until I take you off of it. You'll eat it when you get hungry."

After 20 days, a PA (Physician's Assistant) came to see me and weighted me and took my blood pressure. He told the guards I was still healthy but that they should put me back on regular food. They refused. I continued to work out this whole time, so I was losing weight from 190 pounds fast.

After 27 days on this hunger strike, I was down to 135 pounds, and again The PA told them to feed me regular food. He also told me if I didn't start to eat soon I may not be able to eat when I wanted to.

At 34 days, the PA weighted me in at 123 pounds. He told the guards I was not critical yet, but that I would go critical in the next couple days, if they didn't feed me. Then they would have to feed me through a vein. They refused. The PA took it upon himself to inform the Superintendent of his findings.

The Superintendent passed down the word that I was to be fed anything I would eat, anytime I asked for, so for about a month I had it going on. Peanut butter sandwiches and a carton of milk any time I wanted, oranges, scrambled eggs and sausage or bacon, all I had to do was push a call button. CO Black hated life. Yep, it was great. I had won yet another battle. I was putting weight back on, but I couldn't eat a big meal. A few bites would fill me up, so I end up eating like 6 times a day.

About three weeks went by and I had tricked a graveyard guard into giving me a radio. CO Black had been trying to get the radio back for about a week, threatening me. I was playing it loud and long. Now, on the outside of every cell is a switch that will shut off the power to the cell. For 7 days I am playing this radio and giving them hell. Not a man jack was smart enough to flip the switch and shut off my power.

Every day, CO Black would come and threaten me, but he was just too damn stupid to flip a switch and too damn scared to come in and try to take the radio by force.

At the end of the month I weighted about 135 to 140 pounds and Finishing School was done with me.

One morning, a Correctional Officer came to my door and said "Thorson, cuff up."

I said "Forget it, you ain't coming in"

"Cuff up, your transferring"

"Yeah right, go pull that one on your Momma, boy, because you ain't got no sucker here. You have to come up with something better than that to get into my cell.

"I am serious."

"Show me the paperwork"

He replies "Ok," and he walks out into the sally port and comes right back in with the transfer papers and slips them under the door. I look and it shows I am transferring to W.C.C. (Washington Correction Center at Shelton WA.)

I still don't believe him, but I want it to be true, so I cuff up.

It was true, in a half hour I was on the Chain Bus headed for W.C.C. and away from that sadistic bastard CO Black.

Chapter Twenty Three

I get to Shelton and they put me in the R-Units because they have never had anyone transfer from IMU to the R-Units before. I am put in R3 which is where transfers are supposed to go, but no one has given orders for where I am supposed to go from here.

My cellie is Jerry. He is a great guy, just a dope fiend. He is coming back in on another drug bust. He has done time before. At night, as a part of my work out routine, I sit on the floor as we talk, hitting the concrete with my fists in a rhythmatic pattern to make them hard. We are on the second floor and I hit hard enough to make a small vibration sound. I don't think anything of it because we are talking. Jerry asks "Doesn't that hurt when you hit the floor?"

I reply "No, but when you first start you have to hit lighter until your hands toughen up, but after a while they get pretty hard."

The next day, we are waiting in line for breakfast and the guy in front of Jerry asks "Did you hear that weird vibration sound last night? I wonder what that was."

Jerry replies "It was Thor, doing his Katas."

Dude says "No way. The floor was vibrating, what was he doing?" I was standing right there behind Jerry, so I kneeled down and started hitting the floor with my fists, making the same rhythmatic sound.

Jerry says "He was toughening his fists" as everyone stopped to watch me.

More than one guy said "Damn!" I do the splits and a couple crescent kicks. IMU has put me in the best shape of my life. All I had to do was eat and work out I am still under weight but in good shape.

Well, a week goes by and still, no orders about what to do with me, so W.C.C. calls W.S.P. and DOC in Olympia.

W.S.P. says I was never supposed to be let out of isolation.

Shelton tells me they are going to put me back in IMU. Well, I am going to give them a reason and they know it. I will not go quietly into the night. I will not go without a fight. People are going to get hurt, maybe even me. Stories will be told of this night deeds.

They don't come for a few hours. I am prepared. I will take some of them down and go down fighting to be sure, but none will leave the battle field unscathed. Poor Jerry doesn't know what to do. He will join me in combat, not because he wants to, but because it is the right the thing to do. We are warriors and in my mind it will always be us against them. Jerry wants to be seen as a warrior in my eyes and my opinion counts to him.

They sent one guard. He is like 70 years old. They are cowards to toss this old man to the wolf like that. I would have taken on 10 'warrior class' guards, but my Honour won't allow me to fight an old man, so I go quietly into the night, I go quietly without a fight. My Honour bruised but intact, and Jerry is spared from a decision he didn't want to make.

Well, I was entombed in another Supermax. Now, W.C.C was the place they normally kept kids that had non-violent crimes or were just not deemed strong enough to survive in the other two prisons. (Yes, two prisons. Back then, this state only had 3 prisons) It was considered a cake walk by prisoners in the other two prisons. No big walls here, just the cyclone fences and a couple rolls of razor wire.

When I get into the Supermax there, it was different. It does seem that the more sadistic, small minded, petty guards tended to apply for the positions in the Supermaxs, because in the Supermax, they could get away with more abuses of authority without censure, because usually no one would believe the prisoners allegations of abuse and the prisoners are always handcuffed in the presence of Correctional Officers.

Well, the second day I am there, one prisoner up stairs is beating on his door and kicking the door non-stop. I yell up to him, "Hey, what's going on dude?"

He says he wants to make a phone call. Well, I know better than to ask for anything from the guards as I don't want to give them the satisfaction of turning me down, so I tell the kid, "Dude, they aren't going to give you a phone call, you're just wasting your time."

He tells me "Shut the fuck up. You don't know what you're talking about."

I don't say anything. I figure he will find out the hard way. About 20 minutes later a guard comes on the intercom in his cell. We can all hear it, and asks the inmate what he wants. He tells them a phone call and the guard says "Ok, give me 5 minutes and I'll get you into the yard for a 15 minute call." I am shocked. I have never seen the like. Then I find out that since it is mostly young kids here, they are treated a little differently than I am used to.

But for every up side there must be a down side too I guess.

There is a Correctional Officer that works here named Adams. He is about 27 years old stands about 6'3" 220 pounds, he is a Crow Indian. What he likes to do is to get some mouthy teenager out in the yard and beat him down. Well, CO Adams is picking his fights wisely as he doesn't want to lose a fight. He finds the kids that are skinny and have good heart but can't fight a lick and takes them to the yard then beats them up.

I watch this a couple times and I start getting angry. I start talking shit to CO Adams and talking about his momma, too. I want my shot at him in the yard. I have been putting weight back on pretty quick, going to yard, doing 20 pull ups in a set and 10 sets and using the larger yard to do my Katas in. I must be about 160 pounds and no fat. I am ripped because I have not stopped working out all day, so all the weight I have put back on has just gone to muscle. Well, CO Adams is talking shit back but won't go to the yard with me. I am calling him a coward. Other inmates are telling me that CO Adams isn't a coward. I tell them let him speak for himself and let his actions speak louder than his words.

He won't take my challenge. When I do go to yard one day and my yard time is up, CO Adams comes and tells me to cuff up. I tell him "Come in here and make me cuff up, sissy boy." He again demands that I cuff up. I tell him "Come on in, Sissy, if you're not afraid. You can prove to all these little inmates in here that you're not the coward I say you are." He slams the cuff port and goes and gets the Goon Squad. Now, the yard is a wedge shaped thing with the cinder brick walls covered in stucco, so when the goons come and we do our little dance I get all skinned up on the stucco. Aside from that, not much damage is done on either side.

I am telling all the little kids that been beat up by this sadistic bastard that he is a coward and only fights when he is sure he can win. I knew convicts that built their reps like that. Remember Lewis? Enough said.

I figure I won't even be asked if I want yard the next day. Kid's prisons never cease to amaze me.

The next day I am asked if I want yard again. I say "Yep". We have a repeat of the day before. CO Adams still won't fight me. He never does. He was just a punk with a stick up his butt.

I get written up for refusing to obey a direct order and a couple other rule violations. I plead guilty like it doesn't really matter to me, and tell LT. Olsen hearing the infractions that I can't believe the pussy guards he has working here.

On the way back to my cell after the hearing, I am being walked by a Black Sergeant and a white CO. The Black Sergeant has my arm and is squeezing my tricep real hard trying to cause a little pain. He is about 5'8", 180 pounds, wearing jerry curls and way too much perfume, but is a well muscled guy looking to be in better than average shape, a real sharp looking guy.

I say "Lighten up, Sarg. I won't run away."

"We are all pussies, huh? You're lucky you didn't challenge me, I would have broken you off like a little bitch."

"In your dreams nigger, anytime you want to try me let me know,"

"What did you say?"

"Just like a stupid nigger, can't understand english."

Just then we are passing what is known as a strip cell. The sergeant tells the white guard "Put him in there." This is a room probably 15 foot by 15 foot. The guard opens the door and we all go inside. The sergeant then tells the white guard "Uncuff him!" the guard says "Policy says he must be cuffed anytime he is out of his cell unless in a secured area." The sergeant says "I am giving you a direct order. I didn't ask you what the policy said."

The guard does as he is told. I am thinking two to one odds, I am good with this. I have dealt with greater odds.

Then the sergeant says to the guard "Step outside, Mr. Thorson and I have some things to discuss in private." The guard knows me and starts to protest. The sergeant says "Did you hear me, step outside now!" the poor guard does as he is ordered. Then the sergeant stands facing me with his legs spread wide and his hands on his hips in the typical Superman pose.

The sergeant then says to me. "Now you want to say that again?" I just ain't the talkative sort, I guess, because I just reach out and kick him squarely in the nuts and hit him with a tiger punch that splits his cheek wide open. He folds into the corner crying for help. The white guard is still outside the door and not coming in, but he did the smart thing, as soon as he got outside the door he hit his panic button so help is arriving in record speed.

They wait until like 5 of them are out there and then open the door.

Man, there is one guy 6'5", 450 pounds I am betting, I don't know if he was Samoan or Oriental, but not a lot of fat on this troll. He is the first one through the door. I side kick him in the ribs and then drive my fists as deep into his ribs as I can about 5 times. He then grabs me by coverall front and leg then lifts me over his head and body slams me into the concrete. I would like to tell you how I got up and kicked his big ugly ass, but that story never happened. They dog piled on me and beat me bloody.

Not the sergeant though. As soon as the door opened he ran to the hospital looking to get the 4 inch gash I ripped in his face with my fists patched up. It left a nasty scar because it was ripped flesh, not cut. The goons hand cuffed me and drug me down the hall back to my cell. Now, this sergeant had a reputation in this IMU for fighting prisoners just like CO Adams. Everyone said he was tough, but there is always someone out there who can stomp a mud hole in your ass and walk it dry. If you keep looking you will find him.

He had to come to work with this big ole patch of gauze on his face, so word got around someone kicked the pedestal out from under him.

Well, three days later, I go to the infraction hearing. The hearing officer, LT. Olsen says to me "Thorson, how did you get those handcuffs off?"

"The guard took them off me."

The LT. is mad and he says "Don't play with me, I need to know how you got them off, did you have a paper clip or something?"

"If I did, I wouldn't tell you, but the guard took them off me, for real."

"We will find out," he calls the guard in, and says "Did you notice how Inmate Thorson got out of the cuffs?"

The guard says "Yes Sir, I took the cuffs off of Inmate Thorson, as directed."

"Don't you know the policy?"

"Yes, sir."

"Then, would you mind telling me why you took the cuffs off Inmate Thorson while he was not in a secured area?"

"I was given a direct order to do so by the sergeant in charge."

"Ok, you can go, send the sergeant in on your way out."

"Sergeant, you gave an order for Inmate Thorson to be uncuffed in an unsecure area. Would you mind explaining you're logic in this decision and telling me why you would break policy like that?"

"Inmate Thorson called me a nigger, sir"

"What?"

"He called me a nigger, sir"

"Ok sergeant, you can go, Inmate Thorson as much as I hate to do this, Case Dismissed!"

But aside from that rough beginning the rest of the next year I spent in IMU was pretty uneventful. Around august of 1987 I was sent back to my parent institution W.S.R.

Chapter Twenty Four

May it ever be so humble there is no place like Home.

Well, I hate to say it, but I sure was glad to be back there. I had lived there longer than any other place on earth. The familiar gray walls were beginning to feel a lot like home to me. I no longer really remembered what the streets were like. This is all I know, this is my world. My family hasn't visited me since 1979, I call them on occasion, and my siblings have moved and left no forwarding address. They told my mom to not give me their phone numbers. Only my mom accepts calls from me, but even she didn't visit. So these bleak walls had become home and some of these dangerous men are my brothers, tried and true in the heat of life and death battles. I no longer kept track of time nor did I think about the streets, except maybe in the dreamy way that Christians think of heaven. A nice place but I'll probably never see it again, legally.

I went in to see who my Counselor was, I don't know why we had counselors but we did. So I go in and there was Sergeant Schaller. Schaller is a typical Jewish guy with a mop of black curly hair, schlock nose and black rim glasses. We never got along really. Well guess what? Sergeant Schaller has become a counselor and not just any counselor, he is my counselor. That sucks big time because now I have to ask him for anything I want and we have never got along. I tell Schaller I want a new counselor, he says there is nothing we can do about it he doesn't want me on his case load either, but we will have to make the best of it.

On my first 6 month review with Mr. Schaller, he writes on it "Mr. Thorson appears to be a model prisoner at times, but any one that knows him, knows he is a royal pain in the ass."

I grieve him and make him rewrite that to say "pain in the neck."

I barge into his office to discuss this with him and ask why he would write such a thing about me. He says "Mr. Thorson, if I ordered a whole train box car full of assholes and opened it and found only you inside I would consider that order filled."

I reply "I am sorry to hear that, but I understand you having an attitude."

He says "You do, huh?"

"Yes sir, I would have a bad attitude too, if God had put pubic hair all over my head" and laughed out loud in his face.

He starts screaming in a high pitched girly voice, "Get out of my office! Get out of my office!"

The next day I had Counselor Yost as a counselor. He is a Jew too, but I liked him.

Laws change on a regular basis around here. I don't pay a lot of attention to the laws. The new SRA (Sentencing Reform Act of 1981 AKA The new guidelines) came in around 1984 and was suppose to apply to everyone, and abolish the Board of Prison Terms and Paroles. It was suppose to make everyone's sentence determinate and do away with parole. All old guideline offenders were suppose to be resentenced under the new guidelines. This would have let me out of prison in 1988. But the Parole Board somehow manipulated the legislation and is still around today in 2011. Saying that it was the felons' right to have them, so the legislation said they could keep their job until the last of us was paroled. The parole board came back and resentenced everyone under their jurisdiction to the maximum sentence, thereby giving themselves job security for the next 20 years. No one got parole as everyone was maxed out, old guidelines prisoners did 20 years for the same crime SRA inmates did 5 years for.

With the new laws that passed in 1989, it did cause 3 of my terms to be run concurrent, both assaults and the escape stemming for the 1980 Mason county escape. It, also, gave us a new point system for custody levels.

In November of 1989, I scored minimum custody and so someone decided I should be in a DNR (Department of Natural Resources) Camp.

Now for those of you who don't know, all those guys that are planting trees for Weyerhaeuser and Cascade lumber and fighting forest fires or picking up litter on the side of the road, 95% or more are convicted felons just working their way out of prison. Before you judge a felon to hard, remember it may have been felons giving their life to save your cabin in the woods.

Now, the flip side to that is, these felons are out in the woods 5 days a week and are in the city parks picking up litter 5 days a week, so if they chose to, they can just walk off.

With my escape history and more than ten years to go before I can hope to get out legally, this is where they are going to send me. If I escape, whose fault is it? If you had a dog that killed chickens every chance he gets, and you set him to guard the hen house… what do you expect him to do? Is it really the dog's fault if you tempted him?

I am working in the plumbing shop at this time and I like it. It only pays like 45 dollars a month, but that's pretty average for this time period in the joint. I have no idea about the law change and don't care because I don't think it is going to affect me in any case. I go to my 6 month review and they tell me I score minimum custody and what camp do I want to go to? I tell them "I am not going. I will pass. I have a good job and my wife lives close by, so I'll just stay here."

They tell me that is not an option. I have to go to camp because I score minimum custody.

I tell them "If you send me to camp, I will just escape." They say that is not their problem, they just have to decide which camp to send me to and after that, what I do when I get there is out of their hands.

"If I lose my custody, then do I have to go to camp?"

"No, if you lose your custody you can't go to camp."

"If I quit my job and refuse to work would that make me lose my custody?"

"Yes."

"Ok, I quit."

"What?"

"Ok, I quit my job as of now and I refuse to work anywhere else."

"Thorson, you're going to camp, just give it a chance, you might even like it."

I go out to my boss, Bob, and tell him I quit. He says "what? Why?" So I explain to him about the new custody point system and he says ok he will infract me for quitting and hire me back as soon as I get this thing settled.

I go to the infraction hearing and the hearing officer says "Thorson, you're going to camp. Case dismissed." Is this beginning to look like a conspiracy to anyone else or am I just paranoid?

I go back to me cell to wait for the order to roll it up. Week goes by and one morning a guard comes by my cell and wakes me up.

He says "Thorson, report to the kitchen for a job."

I tell him "Fuck off. I ain't working in no fucken kitchen. Now get the fuck away from the front of my cell."

A little while later he is back, "CUS (Custody Unit Supervisor) Woodley said to tell you to get out of bed and report to the kitchen. That is a direct order."

I say, "Tell Woodley to kiss my ass," and the guard leaves.

Pretty soon the guard is back with CUS Woodley in tow. Woodley says, "I am giving you a direct order to report to the kitchen for work."

I tell him "Look, I don't take orders from no one. I am not going to work in the kitchen. I will do whatever I want to do and if that happens to coincide with your rules, fine, but if it doesn't I personally don't give a damn."

"You can go to work or you can go to the hole. The choice is yours," He says.

"Ok, I'll go to the hole. It isn't anything but another cell, Woodley. I ain't losing anything by being down there. I'll still be in prison."

They come and march me off to the hole. They write me up for refusing a job assignment and disobeying a direct order. My boss comes down to see me and asks me how much longer do I think it will take to lose my custody. I tell him I have it covered and I will be back to work in about two weeks.

I am raising hell with the guards down in the hole keeping them awake all night and talking bad to them during the day.

I go to my infraction hearing and plead guilty to all charges.

The hearing officer says "Ok, well, on both accounts I find there isn't enough evidence to support your claim, so I am dropping the refusing a direct order to inappropriate behavior and dismissing the other charge. I am giving you a reprimand and warning. You're still going to camp, Thorson."

The chain bus comes and they say "Thorson, roll it up you're going to camp."

"I pass, I am not going."

They say "Seriously, roll it up."

"Well, I hope you have the extraction squad warmed up because I am doing my stretches now."

"Seriously, you'll fight not to go?"

"Yep."

"Ok, stand down. I am scratching your name from the list."

CUS Woodley comes down and says "You can go to work in the kitchen and we will let you out of the hole or we are transferring you to Walla Walla."

"Walla Walla doesn't scare me, I'll take Walla Walla, because, I am not working in the kitchen."

The next week the chain bus came and I was on it headed back to Walla Walla via Shelton of course.

I get to Shelton (WCC) and I am put into one of the R-Units and who do I see? CO Adams. Remember him from IMU? He wanted to pick his fights, didn't want to meet me in the yard? I have minimum custody and I really don't want to mess it up, but that doesn't mean I can't fuck with his mind a little, right?

CO Adams is standing by the dining room exit where we dump our trays before leaving. I catch his eye as soon as I stand up. I start walking right towards him like I might hit him with the tray, my eyes locked on his. I know his sphincter puckered up tight, because he had talked a lot of shit to me during the year I was in IMU, but he always stayed behind one of those big iron doors, so was safe. He never saw a time where he might have to back up all that shit talk. Well, now I am walking right up on him and you can see the fear in his eyes, but at the last possible moment I turned and put my tray away. I never said a word to him, but he was more than a little frightened now. I did this to him every time I saw him somewhere.

Well, on the third night, I was brought to the sergeant office in cuffs. I go in and sit down. The sergeant says "Mr. Thorson, do you have a problem with one of my officers?"

"One? No, heck dude, I hate them all."

"Well, what about Officer Adams?"

"Well, yeah, he is more of a punk then most."

"What did you do to him?"

"Nothing."

"Well, I guess we will just find out wont we?"

"Guess so, if you say so, Boss."

The sergeant then tells the clerk to send in CO Adams. The door opens and in comes CO Adams and he stands right behind me. Trying to intimidate me, I guess. The Sergeant then questions CO Adams. "Ok, Officer Adams, would you like to tell me what Inmate Thorson is doing to you?"

"He keeps looking at me," CO Adams says.

The Sergeant says, "And?"

"Well, that's it. He keeps looking at me in an intimidating way."

I say, "If you're that timid maybe you shouldn't be working here."

The sergeant says, "Thorson, that enough."

Then he tells Adams that he could leave he would talk to him later. He didn't like being made to look like a fool by one of his officers being such a pussy.

Adams leaves and the sergeant says, "You've got an attitude problem, how would you like to go to IMU?"

"I'm good with it. I like IMU, single man cell with room service."

"Well, you're scheduled to leave tomorrow on the chain, so try to stay out of trouble!"

"Yeah, right, Can I go now?"

"Officer Baker, take the cuffs off Thorson and send him back to his cell, and tell Officer Adams to report to my office." Man, I would have liked to be a fly on the wall for that conversation.

Chapter Twenty Five

In the morning, it is Christmas Eve, so the chains that would normally be running tomorrow are going today, because no chains run on Christmas. We are all shackled up and put on a chain bus. As we are going down the road, we turn south on I-5.

The guy sitting next to me starts talking excitedly about going to camp at Larch Mountain DNR Camp and starts asking other folks if anyone had been there before and what were we to expect when we got there. He asks me and I say "No," and I am not going to camp with him, I am on my way to Walla Walla. The whole bus falls silent for a moment. Then one of the felons says that everyone on this bus is going to camp. The Walla Walla chain doesn't leave Shelton until next week, it had been cancelled.

I yell at the guard up front and tell him there is a mistake. I am on the wrong bus. I am supposed to be going to Walla Walla. He asks my name and number. I give it to him and he says "Sorry to inform you this Thor, but you're going to camp."

Shit, tricked again! Well, we would see who had the last laugh. So I started asking questions. How high was the fence and where were the towers? No fence and no towers? Wow, and they are sending me here? This must be either a mistake or a set up. Even looking back on it, I can't see the logic of sending me to a place like that. Maybe they needed me to do something so they could use it to get the law changed. I don't know but it was one of those things that make a felon go hummm.

Anyways, the felons click to where my questioning is leading and tell me "Thor, there is no better place to do time, even if it is 11 years at camp. Camp is fun." I am not really swayed by this argument. I figure, if you don't think about escaping at least once a day, you're already dead. I have no intentions of being a willing captive.

I know the United States Constitution died when the right to keep and bear arms was infringed, all your and my freedoms are now just dreams of what used to be. We no longer have our constitutional rights, but that's how it all starts. First you gave up a few of your rights to stop felons from having those rights, but you don't have those rights anymore either. You're losing your right to keep and bear arms real soon watch.

But in any case, I consider it my right, as a human being, to escape from captivity every chance I get and I won't give up that right. In Mexico, there is no law against escaping from prison. It is thought to be a god given right. So I have no intention of staying once I get off the bus. I will take a couple days and case the place, get the lay of the land and then I am out of there.

We go up these winding roads deep in the woods and the black guys are all asking about bear attacks. The whites and Mexicans are laughing at them. Africans Americans afraid of animals where are their natural jungle instincts? Not too many blacks last at DNR camps unless they land in-camp jobs. Mostly because they are afraid of bears and too lazy to give a good days work in the field, so the Crew Bosses won't take them out more than once or twice. Now, if they land a kitchen or laundry job they do just fine.

Well, we all unload from the chain and get unshackled. The Sergeant, Aerosmith, looks us over and says "Which one of you is Thorson? "

I say "I am"

"Come with me," we go into a small room with two other guards and he says strip and gives me some blue coveralls to wear. Then he tells the other two guards "Put Mr. Thorson in The hole he is going back on the first thing smoking, next week."

I think cool; it was all a mistake, so I sit out Christmas Eve and Christmas in the hole. They try to bring me some cake and treats. I tell them keep it, I don't believe in all that crap anyway and I don't want the state saying they did me any favors or treated me good.

The day after Christmas, I get called out to the sergeant's office and he has a piece of paper there in front of him. He says "Mr. Thorson, promise me you won't try to escape and I will let you out of the hole and you can stay here."

"My word is good for you?"

"Yes, Mr. Thorson, I believe you're a man of your word. Give me your word and sign here and you can stay here."

"Ok, you have it, I ain't going no place," now in my mind I am thinking, my word to a guard… ain't any way I have to keep that and I am out of here in a couple days. So I sign his little promissory note.

Then he says "Ok, go to breakfast, and then report to the property room to get your clothes."

So as I am going to breakfast and I see two life size deer statues on the lawn. I say "What stupid ass put them dumbass statues there?" to no one in particular. Then one of the deer turns its head to look at me. I am awe struck, I say "My Gawd they're real." The felon standing next to me says "Yeah and if you have an apple or cookie they will eat right out of your hand." So I hurry and go eat and save my apple. Then when I come out of the dining hall, I offer it to the nearest one and sure enough she stretches her neck out and takes it from my hand. Right then this big fat Correctional Officer tells me "You! In the office right now!" So I go in there and he says "What were you told about feeding the deer?"

"I wasn't told anything"

"Yes you were! You were all told at orientation not to feed the deer"

"I never went to orientation"

"Don't give me that shit, you were there, I remember you"

Right then Sergeant Aerosmith says "No Savajoe, Thorson wasn't there, he was in the hole. Thorson, you're not to feed the deer while you're here, now go pick up your property."

That was my first run in with Savajoe, who we renamed Sloppy Joe for his fat unkempt manner. But him and another asshole guard named Younse were always trying to find dirt on someone or other and were always trying to set prisoners up for failure. Their greatest enjoyment was watching someone get sent back to medium custody that they had set up. Everyone knew that too, so tried to avoid the assholes.

After seeing the deer, I was willing to give this place a shot. I like animals and hadn't seen any in a long time. During my stay at Gladiator School, I had taken a horticulture class just to be around the plants. But there were no trees inside the walls and here I could go hug a tree. Sepida was there and caught me hugging a tree. He knew what I was going through. So he teased me calling me a tree hugger. There was snow on the ground of course. It would come and go being at that elevation.

My first week went pretty smooth and I decide I like this place so I will just stay after all. I get called out to go on DNR and I am on Bucks Black Sheep Crew. All the crews have names and 'Black Sheep' suited me just fine.

Now up to this point, I had never used a chain saw and was a little afraid of them because I had seen the damage they inflict when used wrongly on TV. The prisons are full of loggers and ex-Military people, but Alderman and Dyer showed me the ropes. After about a week the boss, Buck, told me to take a chain saw and go cut down a stand of alders, about 8 trees as big around as your thigh.

Now, the whole time I have been on the crew I have been preaching about how this is not replanting the forests as there are no hard wood trees that supply food for the deer and elk. I am gung ho to plant trees to save the world from bad air quality. I am a tree hugger for sure.

I go and cut down all those alder trees. I 'accidently' hit the ground with the chainsaw running and probably dulled the chain. I go back to Buck and say "Ok, Boss, I murdered all of those trees, but I fucked up my weapon."

He said "Well, I don't have another saw for you, so you just pack gas for Alderman alright?"

"Sure."

So that's what I do for a while, then we actually get some trees to plant and they give us some saddle bags that fit around your waist to pack these little seedlings in. Now most of the guys, I can see right off, are slackers. They are barely taking a handful in each side. Not me, I am here for this. I have a mission to plant trees and save the world. So I pack trees into both sides and I pack those bags full. No one tells me anything they just watch. Then they head out, me too. After like 5 minutes I realize why the rest of the crew are slackers. My hips are being rubbed raw by the canvass saddle bag and the movement of walking. I am considering digging a big hole and making it a grave for a bunch of these trees. But just then, one of the guys is going back for more trees. Instead of going to the truck he comes to me and says "Can I have some of your trees?" and he reloads his bags.

He doesn't take much, so I am still thinking about dumping some trees. Then here comes another guy, and another. So the crew was glad I had packed their reloads halfway up the mountain for them. Next day I knew better.

Tree planting is over and we are back to thinning trees. Buck likes to get drunk out there in the woods. One day he disappears and is nowhere to be found at quitting time, he must have passed out somewhere. We decide while we are waiting we might as well do a hobby hunt, cut burls from trees to take back to the prison hobby shop and make clocks and other cool things from the burl wood. We get done and still no Buck, so we start honking the truck horn. Now here comes Buck, he is not in a good mood. He steps up into the back of the crummy (truck) where the felons ride and says "Who told you guys to come out of the woods? No one leaves their job post unless I say they do."

One of the guys tried to explain it was quitting time. Then Buck sees all the hobby wood and says no one is getting paid today and all the hobby wood he was going to give to another crew. Then he says "And if anyone of you pusses have a problem with that, step off the bus right now and I will kick your ass!"

I stand right up and start heading for the door. But Buck is quick to say "That doesn't apply to you, Thor. It was the rest of the crew I was talking to, because they knew better." He shuts up and we get on the way back. Now, Buck is drunk and driving fast. I think he got lost or took a wrong turn because all of a sudden he locks up the brakes and turns the truck into the mountain side. The truck stops sideways across the road and I look out my window on the passenger side at where a road had been before the dirt slide had took out the road and left a 150 foot drop.

Everyone gets out and we direct a see-saw motion to get the truck back on the road going back the way we had come. In the mean time

I take out my camera that the camp allows you to buy and I get some great pictures of an elk herd watching us from the valley below.

When we make it back to camp, Buck pulls me aside. Now normally we make 25 cents an hour with the "nut sack" (lead man) making 45 cents an hour on a DNR crew. Well Buck told the whole crew they were not getting paid for today's work, but he tells me "Thor, today you're the only one getting paid and I am paying you 45 cents an hour." So I tell him "Tomorrow I am taking a chain saw and I am tired of packing gas and Alderman will pack gas for me he said, if there are not enough saws to go around."

Right then Buck says "No, you're not carrying a chain saw."

I am offended and say "Yes, I am."

Buck says "No one that calls a chainsaw a weapon and murders things with it will ever carry a chain saw on my crew!"

So from that day forward Buck never called me out to his crew again. The other crew boss' would take me out, but only if one of their crew was sick. I found a job opening in the ground maintenance crew and worked there. That was really cool because I could then go past the boundary signs and go down to the creek and fish for trout. I had to release them and all I had was some line and a few hooks tied to a stick, but I saw where the red belly newt lived and I enjoyed just sitting out in the woods all alone and far enough away from the camp to not hear the sounds.

I worked there for about 3 months. I knew more than the boss about plants and how to condition the soil. The boss got me any plants I wanted and other things, like lime to sweeten the soil and sand and peat moss which I turned into the soil where the garden patch was. It was great I was really enjoying my time here at this camp.

Well, it is 6 month review time again. Remember that's what got me into this mess? I go in, prepared to tell them, yep, I like it here. They have seen how I turned a few mud holes into awesome flower beds and rejuvenated a few old ugly shrubs into works of art. I don't foresee any problems.

I go in and sit down. Apparently DOC in Olympia has figured out keeping felons at camp with long term sentences doesn't make good sense.

Usually as soon as they tell a felon he is going back to an institution they toss him in the hole, but usually a felon going back has been a troublesome felon. I am an easy keeper, if you don't go out of your way to hassle me.

They tell me I am going back. I can see they are watching for my reaction. So I reply "Do you think they will send me back to WSR?"

They say "Maybe, if that is where you came from, why?"

"That's where all my friends are. Do you want me to go pack my stuff now?"

They look at each other and you can see their minds work. Poor sap is institutionalized and he will save us the job of packing his stuff. We can toss him in the hole after he packs his stuff.

They say "Sure go pack your stuff and bring it up to the property room to be inventoried."

I say "OK."

I go pack all my stuff and then instead of taking it anywhere I put on three pairs of jeans and three shirts my navy pee coat and purple scarf. Take a couple books of matches and some cookies I stole from the kitchen at lunch. I step out the window and hit the woods.

Chapter Twenty Six

It is around April 15th I think and still cold outside and being up on a mountain there is still snow in places. But I am bundled up pretty good.

I decide to head south as best I can as Oregon is that direction and the Colombia River is on the border. I don't know how far it is but I am not real concerned. I have spent a lot of my time reading about what plants are edible in the wild.

Well as I start to cross the creek on this log during the night I slip and fall in. I am soaked to the bone, now it is cold for sure. But I get out on the far bank and just start marching. I figure if I walk far enough and fast enough I will keep warm. But after about an hour I am still climbing up in altitude and I hit the snow line. I know this isn't going to work. Not with my clothes all wet. So I decide to just head down hill in any direction that will take me. I just want to be somewhere that is warmer.

Well by noon I still don't see anything but woods and I am exhausted and freezing. I know hypothermia makes you want to sleep and I am tired. My cookies are mush, I eat them anyways and my matches are dissolved so no fire. I sit down and think 'should I just go back? Then instantly I answer myself hell no I would rather die free in the woods than live caged'. So I sit down by a tree and prepare to just die. I pass out from the cold and exhaustion. I wake up and it is daylight, I forgot I was dying and I just start moving. I see what appears to be a castle out in the woods but there are cars and things there. So I start heading toward it thinking I will be able to steal some food and maybe a car. Takes me hours to get close to it and as I get close it disappears. But that's OK because just a little farther on is a Bar, and someone probably will have left their keys in the car. So I start making my way towards the bar. It is almost dark by the time I get close. But the bar soon too disappears. So I know now that I am hallucinating. So I sit down. I see a barn up ahead but it will have to wait as I know it's not real. So I just sit down and figure this time when I go to sleep it will be my last time for sure. But I am too tired to care. So I go to sleep. I wake up just before sun rise and get up and start heading towards the barn knowing it is not real but having no other goals and no place else to go.

But the barn was still there when I got there. Man, I could have slept inside last night. I finally found civilization so I go into the barn and look around. There is a new truck in the barn so I figure I will steal it. I get inside and nothing looks like anything I know. The newest car I had been in up to this point was a 1971 Ford. This is a Ford but a 1989 or 91. So I realize I can't steal this truck. But on the seat is a bag full of chocolate foil wrapped foot ball's (Easter eggs) and a tin of sugar cookies. I wolfed the cookies down one right after another and put the footballs in the pockets of my pee coat. I was going to just walk away when I saw a 10 speed bike in the bed of the truck. I took it out, checked it over and got on it and down the road I went.

I had no idea where I was or where I was going but I was going as far as I could.

I road for about an hour and found the Vancouver Mall in Vancouver Washington. So I pulled in and found a phone booth. I made a collect call to my wife Annette and told her I needed a ride. She called one of my ex-cell partner David and told him to come get me. She gave him her credit card and told him to rent a car and get whatever he thought I would need.

Let me break from the story here to say Annette is a saint. She let like 5 or 6 guys parole out to her from prison because all they needed was an address. She got them cars and let them stay until they were ready to be on their own. That's how and why she had the recourses and know how to help me.

So mean while David is taking his time dicking around getting loaded guns and stuff.

Well in the Mall parking lot the security is wondering who I am sitting on their sidewalk and dozing off. I look like I haven't bathed in months. So they come ask me who I am and what am I doing there. I am sure they think I am homeless and panhandling. So I give them a story and a fake name. They leave but they called the cops. I was just riding my bike around when I notice three squad cars pulling into the parking lot so I head for a bit of bushes across the street and lay the bike down and I lay down behind the bushes the security is showing the cops where I was and they do a little drive around. I stay put for like an hour. Then I ride away and go to the freeway on ramp and head north to Seattle. I stick my thumb out and someone stops right away. Man I am relieved to be away from there.

This ride only takes me as far as Longview. So I get out and as it is getting dark I go to the AM/PM mini mart and tell the guy behind the counter that I was hitchhiking up from California and got robbed and dumped in the ditch. That I have no money but could I make a collect call to my friends in Seattle to come and get me?

He says "Sure buddy no problem."

So I call Annette and say "Where the hell are you?"

She then tells me that she thinks the cops are watching her house so she called David and sent him to come get me. But when he got there the place was swarming with cops so he figured I had been picked up. So I give her my new location and tell her to send Dave to get me I was safe in here and would just wait for him.

So I guess Dave calls her again to see if anything is happening when he stops for gas and he isn't too far from where I am. I tell the guy in the store I am hungry and does he mind if I get something to eat on credit? He says I can have some of those little burgers from the deli section. So I go down the line adding everything to the burger because I haven't eaten in a couple days. I never saw a mini mart with a hot deli section before. So I see sliced pickles and add a thick row of them on to my burger then I bite in. man those pickles... were hot peppers. I had to scrap them back off. Live and learn I guess.

About that time David shows up and pays for my snack then asks me if there is one thing you want to have before we leave just in case we get caught what is it? I say "A wine cooler" I been seeing these commercials for Bartle's and James' Wine Coolers for a couple years and wanted to try one. So he went in and bought me a 4 pack of Blackberry Seagram's Seven wine coolers. I drank them one after the other like pop. They tasted so great, like the nectar of the Gods.

So we are on the road again headed north on Interstate 5. David pulls out a .380 and a box of shells and hands them to me. He shows me he has a .9mm for himself. He says just in case we are stopped.

I tell him if we are stopped I will just go back I am not interested in getting into a gun fight with the cops. But I look at it as it is a nice little pistol. He takes me up to Kirkland to the Sherries restaurant just off I-405 at the 116th St. exit. We order food he orders a steak for me but I can't eat the whole thing as my stomach never really recovered from that 35 day hunger strike. So I can't eat big meals. I have to eat small meals more often, but generally I just snack all day. But I still look like something the cat drug in. Then he takes me to the Ramada Inn and checks me in under his name. I take a long hot bath and just soak until the water cools. Then I stand up shower off with hot water again and David had provided a sweat suit top and bottom. So I crawl into that and drop on the bed and crash.

David takes all my clothes and my Navy Pee coat wrap them in garbage bags and tells me he is going to have everything cleaned. He doesn't it sits in his garage like that for about two years I guess. Everything is well molded and rotted by then, it all gets tossed out.

But what do I care? No much I am free! I loved that Pee coat, but hey I am free right? That's all that really matters to me.

I don't find this part out until much later, But David likes to tell stories, he tells folks I got so drunk off those four wine coolers that I passed out and that I tried to take his .380 from him. I protected his dumbass when he was in the joint and if I had wanted to take anything from him, there wasn't a damn thing he would be able to do about it. But aside from being a liar he is a pretty good guy. That being said I will get on with my story.

So I wake up the next morning and call my Mom. Tell her what has happened. She was out of the loop by this time with me calling her rarely. So she was happy to hear I was out again but not so happy at how I had gotten out. She told me to hang around for a day or two and see if she could scare up some ID for me. I asked her about her finding a long lost Aunt and her tribe about 3 years earlier and where they were. She told me hang around for a bit and she would see if she could secure a place for me with them in British Columbia Canada.

So in a few hours she calls me back and says if I can make it there, she has my Aunts address in Kelowna BC for me. So I give this information to my wife and David.

Plans are made I get a haircut and shave my full beard into a long handlebar mustache. Annette is funding this vacation for me. So she has David buy me clothes and whatever else I need, toothbrush etc. David is scalping Annette badly on the money, claiming he spent more than he did and collecting it from her. I am starting not to like David so much anymore.

We stop off at David's house to tell his girl friend Luanne that he will be gone for a day or two. She turns on the tears like he is going off to war and will never come back. She is a real helpless clingy sort of thing. Used to be cute but is getting pretty fat by now. David is treating her bad and messing around with any woman that will give him the time of day. She knows it but is stilling clinging to him like a bad rash. So we finally get away from that bad scene and are on the road heading north.

Now David being the asshole he is wants to cruise past the Prison W.S.R. where I have done most of my time and all the guards know me by face. He was taking a real risk here with my freedom. But he is a thrill seeker and he was driving so there wasn't much I could do short of killing him. Then he takes me to Roslyn WA where Northern Exposure TV series is filmed so I can see it. I guess this is one of his more favorite sitcoms on TV. Me, I could care less I am just trying to stay out of the lime light. So we head over Hwy 2 to Monroe then down 203 to I90 to Roslyn then back up Hwy 97 to Twisp WA, where we hang out waiting for my sister in law Diane at her farm and so David can try to get laid. Don't know if he is successful or not.

But more importantly to me I finally get to meet my sister in-law Diane and my beautiful niece who I have talked to on the phone for about 7 years but never met. Teresa is my favorite niece on that side of the family to this day. But I don't tell them who I am because I don't know how they would react.

So after dinner David and I head for the boarder. Now I don't have any ID. My momma wasn't able to secure any documents for me on such short notice. So as we come within a few miles of the Canadian border David and I make the plan I will lay back in the seat and pretend I'm asleep if I'm asked for ID, I'll reach for it and then search for it and then cuss a blue streak about losing my wallet.

We get to the border and the border guard asks David the nature of his visit and David tells them business. He is the owner of a taxi cab company and there is a convention up in Vancouver we are going to. The border guard says "Why didn't you go up I-5 since you are based out of Seattle."

David says "We have friends we wanted to visit before going to Vancouver."

The Border Guard then says "Who is with you?"

David says "One of my drivers"

"Does he have ID?"

"Yes of course he does, oh the car rental agency said I had to show you these papers when I crossed the Border. Is this all I'll need or is there something more you'll need?"

"No this is it, I'll be right back"

He walks to the border station and David starts to talk to me I tell him shut up I heard it all so just sit there quietly.

Just then the Border Guard comes back and says "Ok enjoy your stay. The speed limit is in Kilometers so keep that in mind and drive safe."

We had made it passed the border!!

Chapter Twenty Seven

We arrive in Kelowna BC about 5:00 AM and we cannot find the address. We drive around for about half an hour but no luck. So we find a little store with a pay phone outside and go in and buy something to eat for breakfast and sit in the car waiting until about 6:30 then I call my aunt and wake everybody up. I ask for directions. But she says just to sit tight and she would send My Cousin Deann Lynn to come get us.

She shows up in about 10 minutes and leads us back to my Aunts place. Here are people I haven't seen since I was 5 years old. It was a great reunion. I had missed the family reunion of 1988 when this lost tribe was found again. This was also the time when the facts about our family heritage came out. My Grandma on my mother's side was a full blooded Oneida Indian. But had been passing for a French Canadian, being born in 1907 Indians were still being hung in a lot of places. Her father was the medicine man. So I grew up already knowing a lot of medicine plants and their uses.

So anyways now here I am and being doted on by all my female cousins and their children. My aunt is making us breakfast. As we wait for breakfast, I tell everyone about how David's girlfriend drove us nuts with her crying like she was sending him off to war and everyone had a good laugh about it.

David has caught the eye of my cousin Patsy. She is a midget about 4'6" and a year older then I am. David having an expense account (Annette's) is playing the big spender and taking everyone out to this little country western bar called The Corral. It is a nice place not too expensive. But when you're treating 4 girls and 2 guys it could get a little pricey.

I am sitting next to my Aunt along the dance floor watching the dancers. There is a lady standing just in front of us and every time she goes to light her cigarette I light it for her. She is about 50. But I think she thinks I am hitting on her, and my Aunt sitting next to me I am sure she thinks is my girlfriend so me and my Aunt are getting a little kick out of this. Now where we are sitting it is bar stools and folks are walking around to and from the dance floor right behind us.

Well this one guy falls into my back as he is walking past and kind of uses my back as a shove off point as he launches himself further down the lane. I turn and say "Excuse me" but he just continues away from me not saying anything. In my mind I am thinking 'you sorry son of a bitch better not do that again'. But in a moment I forget about it and go back to flirting with this older babe. Not 15 minutes later another drunk bumps me or maybe the same one I don't know and starts to walk off as I start to say excuse me I see he isn't going to say anything in return so I step in front of him and grab a handful of shirt and say "Can you spell Pardon Me?

The drunk says "Huh?"

"I said can you spell Pardon Me Mutherfucker? You bumped into me and I think you owe me an apology!" I keep my voice down low and menacing because I don't want to draw attention I just want the respect I think I am owed.

The Drunk says "Oh hey Buddy I am sorry I didn't even notice"

"No problem there buddy I am sorry to I thought you did it on purpose" and the drunk goes on his way. I turn back towards my seat and I see this silver belt buckle big enough to brush your teeth in, and it is chest high. So I look up and there about a foot above my head is a cowboy hat. I figure this must be the drunks back up because he says to me "Is there a problem?"

I say "Not unless you want to start one, your buddy bumped into me and didn't apologize so I just made him mind his manners."

The Giant says "He's not my buddy I am one of the bouncers here, are you a Yank?"

"Hell No I am from The South, Yanks are from up North."

"Well up here we call everyone from the States a Yank."

"So tell me what happened, Yank"

"I ain't no damn Yank. But this guy bumped into me and was going to walk away without apologizing, so I just asked him if he was going to apologize or not and he did so everything is fine. Where I come from folks is polite enough to apologize if they bump into other folks."

"Well Yank, up here folks is mostly real friendly and we don't pay a lot of attention to who is bumping into whom. Maybe it would be a good idea if you and your lady friend take a booth. That way no one is likely to bump into you."

"Ok, but the Lady is My Aunt"

So we moved into a booth and my aunt was looking at me like she didn't know what kind of wild beast had come into her family. She says "What was that all about?"

I said "Just making folks mind their manners."

So the bar is closing but my aunt knows the bar keep and buys some bottles of peppermint schnapps and whiskey to go. So we head on home and continue to party. David and Patsy disappear into a bedroom. Then my aunt goes to bed. My other cousin Shelly goes home. So Deann (pronounced Dee-Ann) and I finish off the bottles and crash on the front room floor. As her two kids have the only other bedroom...

On about the second day I am there my Aunt come to me and says "Robbie Honey do you smoke pot?"

Now I figure she is concerned about my drug use in prison or something so I tell her a little white lie. "Well I have smoked it but not a lot and not anymore."

She then says "Well do you mind if the rest of us do?"

I tell her "you smoke pot?"

"Yes"

"Ok I smoke pot too"

"Oh good will you go down to the basement with Deann and harvest some more while I load the pipe as we are running low."

So I follow my cute cousin down to the basement and she takes down a painting on the wall and pulls on the nail that was holding the painting and that whole section of wood paneling swings open on hinges. Behind the hidden door is a room with lights and pot plants and a drip irrigation system. This is right next to the washer and dryer and the dryer hose also dumps into this room. But that has caused a mildew problem on the nearest plants. But my cousin assures me this has not affected the quality of the pot. So she takes a couple buds that are there and pinches a little of the leaves to keep the height down and to make the plants branch out more. I am amazed to say the least. But I guess the outlaw blood runs deep in my veins all through the Oneida side of my family. I ask Deann about the room and she says my cousin Joey built it when he lived here for a bit.

Well David stays for about 5 days going the bar every night, sleeping with Patsy and just having a good time. He gives me 35.00 dollars and tells me to try to make it last. Well it doesn't last I need cigarettes and they are 5.00 a pack in B.C. opposed to the 3.00 a pack in the USA. So in a day or so I call Annette and ask her if she can wire me any money.

She says "What you're out of money already? David said he left you with 300.00 dollars and I had to give him 700.00 for his expenses too."

I tell her "David let me with 35.00 and some change."

She says "That's ok, don't say anything, I'll see what I can get together and send it up to you."

Now it is true, Annette was making good money back then working for Boeings. But she got David out of prison gave him a place to stay, and got him a car. That he ripped her off like that just isn't right. Until now writing this story I hadn't given it much thought but maybe I'll look David up and make him pay that back or beat his ass.

Anyways David has left and Patsy asks me at dinner, "Do you think he will be back or at least call me?"

I say "Depends on if he can get away from his girlfriend or not."

She says "He has a girlfriend? Why didn't you tell me?

"I did remember the first day we were here and I told you about how his girlfriend was driving us nuts with her whining?"

"Oh you're right, you did tell me but I just forgot."

So she calls him up and makes life a little rough on him asking him questions he doesn't want to answer and so ends another illicit love affair.

Well I get up there around April 18, I figure. I am not real good at dates as time hasn't meant a lot to me in a lot of years. But I stay with my Aunt for a couple months. She breeds Cockatoos in her back room and has a couple pets out in the dining area. Deann has a Quaker parrot named Toby. Toby and I hit it off right away. There are a couple pair of cockatoos in the back room, a Lilac Crown Amazon and a green cheek Conure in the dining room with Toby.

The girl next door Marie, also has a bird collection. She has Cockatiels, Splendid Parakeets, budgies, Eleanor cockatoos, a citron Cockatoo, a Mitre Conure and an African gray. She is a cute Blonde, but more than a little dizzy. So I do spend some time over there. But she is paranoid. I go and tell a guy she is afraid of to back off and leave her alone. But I am not sure he was even doing anything to her. But of course he calls the RCMP. They show up while we are in the back yard. So I duck inside and go into the basement and sit on the floor by a pile of misc stuff she has down there. I sit cross legged with my head tucked between my knees and pull a rug and a lamp shade up on my back. So just look like another pile of junk laying there. Because in Canada the Royal Canadian Mounted Police don't need a search warrant to enter into your home. The officer does come in and do a quick look around and tells Marie if she knows where the guy is that threatened the victim it would be in her best interest to tell him or call when she saw him next. Then he leaves. I am amazed she held her mud (Didn't tell). But now she is a little afraid to have me around. I am like a dangerous toy to her that she gets a thrill by playing with but is afraid of getting hurt by.

After about two months I still have not found work so my Aunt always worrying about where the next buck is coming from tells me I have to move. So I am thinking I will have to go back to the USA. But my Cousin Deann says she is moving out too has found a little place by Lake Okanogan and I can move in with her. So I start going to man power everyday for day jobs and I go to the park at night and collect pop and beer bottles as the stores redeem them for cash. So I do that every morning. Then Deann's boss says he will hire me too on her SIN Number and make it look like she is working two shifts. So life is good. I live 40 feet from a lake that has a sea serpent in it called

Ogopogo. Like the Loch Ness Monster. I never saw it but I looked for it a lot.

So this went along just fine until August 3rd when my boss called and told Deann that the RCMP had called looking for me. He said he would have to let me go and that was that. Now I knew at that time I should just head back to the states. Just drop everything and leave on the run. But I didn't. What a dumbass I can be at times.

So I didn't go anywhere. I figured they didn't know just where I was. I had time to make a plan and I would do that after payday. That night about 3:00 AM the RMCP came busting in, I roll out of bed and squeeze in-between the dresser and the wall and cover myself with dirty clothes trying to look like a pile of dirty clothes waiting to be washed.

The RMCP came in and tossed the bed against the wall and didn't find me. So they were saying things like he is gone and running for sure, and he must have left last night etc. then one of the RMCP in frustration kicked the pile of dirty clothes and hit me then yelled in surprise "He's right here I got him!"

The place I lived only had one door and I told my cousin Deann when we moved in I didn't like it. Hell a rat won't trust a den with only one exit. But the price was right and it was nice. I should have dropped everything and ran when I first heard they were looking for me.

So we get down to the station and I am being interviewed. As part of the interview I am informed of my rights. I have the right to claim Refugee Status if I feel my country is persecuting me instead of prosecuting me. Meaning if I think my country is being unfair to me and if I prove it they won't send me back to the USA. But the RMCP tell me I won't get it. But what the heck I declare I am a refugee. I have nothing to lose.

Chapter Twenty Eight

So I am flown to Vancouver B.C. and lodged in the county jail. I am given a barrister named Linda Mark and we proceed to the refugee status. Meanwhile she is trying to get me transferred to the hotel where other refugees are kept. A less secure place and nicer she says. But I must tell you for a county jail I have never been in a nicer one. As soon as I come out of my cell the first time I see Frank. A guy I knew from Gladiator School in the 1970s. He is an Indian or first people as they are called in Canada.

So we catch up on old times, the Canucks are all listening wide eyed. They had no idea that they had real dangerous folks in their midst. They were all bank robbers or drug dealers. So then Frank goes back to his cell he is doing a county jail bit for selling drugs. So is trying to just sleep as much as possible.

So I start hanging out with the Canucks in the dayroom and a group of us are talking about another one no one likes. So one of these guys say that the other guy we don't like is a Goof. So I say well your kind of a Goof yourself buddy. They all fall silent and are looking from the guy I called a goof to me. Then one of them says "Hey, the yank doesn't know what that means. He didn't mean anything by it."

So I say "What does it mean? As it turns out it is the same as calling someone a punk in the USA Prisons. So I tell them we call folks like that a punk. So they have a great laugh and start going around to other inmates calling them punks and saying come here punk. Then laughing their heads off when the guy does.

So anyways we go to court everyday and we go to yard everyday. Now this whole county jail is state of the art. Everything is controlled from a booth on the main floor. The elevators doors are opened and closed and the destination is controlled from this main control booth.

So when you go to yard the guard hits a keypad combination to open the unit door. Then goes to the elevator door and is on camera. A voice from the ceiling asks the destination the guard says second floor yard. The door opens we all get in and the elevator moves off to its destination.

Well one day the elevator is taking a long time to get to us so the guard being impatient takes us over to the fire escape door and pushes the three digit code to take us down the stairs. Being a smartass I say "Oh great if I make it this far I will burn at the bottom of the stairs when the building falls on me."

The guard says "No you won't just hit the breaker bar on the door at the bottom of the stairs and you are on the streets."

I keep telling the courts that my aunt lives here and will sponsor me and my mom fought in the Royal Canadian Navy during WWII. So I should be shown some consideration. But every time I have them call my aunt for some kind of support she doesn't give it. She must be afraid of what they will do to her for aiding and abetting or she is afraid they will find the pot plants she is growing. So I don't push it.

Now this is an escape proof county jail and the guards are growing lax because it is escape proof. If you don't have the codes you can't get out. Opportunity favors the prepared mind. I watch everything. I memorized the 6 digit key pad to get out of the unit and the three digit code for the fire escape just in case. I tell Frank I may need a diversion if my refugee act doesn't pan out and I explain to him my plan.

During my refugee hearing I am kept with others in a waiting room. There is one from Hong Kong. He is a Tong member and is being deported. But he has taken an interest in my case. So in his broken English he asked me if I was going to try to escape again. I told him of course and told him of my plan and of my other escapes. He gave me 40.00 cash and told me I would need it for clothing and a taxi. When I got out I was to call him and he would arrange for me passage to Hong Kong where he could use a guy like me.

So I ripped a hole in the fly of my boxer underwear and rolled the money up into a tube and slipped in into the double seam of my boxers. I then flattened the tube of money out as much as possible after it was in place.

It passed the search no problem. So a few days later my refugee act failed. My Mom and Aunt Christine show up to help plead my case for staying in Canada. But they are unsuccessful so they are a little distraught.

I was informed that I would be sent back to the border crossing at 6:00 that day and there would be a US Marshal there to take custody of me and if no one was there I would just be released.

So I get back to the unit and tell Frank to get the guard to the back of the unit so I could make my move.

Frank goes to the back of the cell and starts yelling "Oh man! Oh My God!" the guard goes back to see what is going on. I go to the door and punch in the code the door pop's open. I walk out and there is a guard's station between the two units on the ninth floor. The guard in the office looks at me. I give him the nod and walk over in front of the elevator. The guard picks up his newspaper and I walk around the corner to the fire escape door punch in the code in. Down nine flights of stairs I run and hit the breaker bar on the door at the bottom of the steps and I am out on the street in lime green jail clothes that say Vancouver Regional Correctional Centre in white down the legs and across the back. People on the street are looking at me but no one is trying to stop me. It is about 3:30 PM and I have nowhere to go.

Across the street is a big hotel with an underground parking lot. So I head across the street and into the underground parking lot. Then I go to where the stairs are and find a hiding place under the stairs. So I sit there for about an hour or so. Then I decide to go pilfer some cars for whatever I can find. Now as soon as I touch the handle of some cars the interior lights come on. I run away figuring it is the car alarm coming on. But it isn't it is some courtesy thing newer cars have. So I figure that out and go ahead on the mission of finding some clothes or money. I find a pocket knife and some change then I find a pack of cigarettes. I needed a smoke for sure. So I go sit under the stairs for a while and smoke a couple cigarettes. Then I go back and continue my search. I find a baseball cap some sunglasses and a bright red oversized parka made of wind breaker material.

Now my Mom and Aunt were up stairs in the hotel lunch room waiting for the rush hour traffic to ease up before heading home. But I didn't find this out until much later and of course they had no idea that I was on the loose again.

So after about 3 hours go by I figure the search has probably moved on to other areas so I put on my new bright red over sized parka that goes to me knees and covers all or most of the white lettering saying Vancouver Regional Correctional Centre. My plan is to just leave Canada and go back to the USA. So I walk over to a little store and there is a Taxi Cab. So I walk up and tell him I need to go to the border.

He says "How much money do you have?"

I say "40.00 bucks"

He says it will take more than that.

Then he looks at my pants and says "Get in"

I start to get in the back seat and he says "No get in the front." Then he says excitedly with a big smile "You're the Yank that escaped from the jail huh?"

I say "Yep"

So he starts the car up and says "Look I can't take you to the border but the bus will. He calls dispatch and finds out when the bus I want is leaving and where to catch it at. We have about a half hour so he says "I'll give you a tour of our fine city and you tell me about the escape ok?"

So we strike a deal and he is driving around telling me how the call came out over the cab radios to be on the lookout for me. But most of the Cabbies had decided if they saw me they would help me not the RMCP. So he takes me to the bus stop just as my bus is pulling in and gives me a handful of change for the bus and tells me to get off in Whitefish and walk from there.

On the bus I sit in an empty seat near the back. Next stop a bunch of Punk Rockers get on the bus. The first Punk Rockers I have ever seen. A really cute girl with bright red liberty spikes and a black spiked collar sits right next to me. She smells good but I have to smile at the way she is dressed in all bright clashing colors and her heavy black make up, black mini skirt, black fishnet nylons with a hole in the knee lime green vest bright yellow satin like blouse. Earrings in her eye brows lips and nose. I am in love with the moment and the girl instantly. She opens a punk rocker magazine of some sort and is reading it. I am looking at the pictures in her magazine as she turns the pages and just enjoying the moment. I felt like I was looking at some form of exotic butterfly. She turns toward me suddenly and says in a gravelly voice like Linda Blair on the exorcist "You want to read this?"

I reply laughingly "No, I was just looking at the pictures. But thanks for offering. I have never seen Punk Rockers before. You people are awesome."

So she asks where am I going and we had a pretty fun conversation, but before too long she gets off and I am alone again.

I get off a couple stops later and apparently to early as I don't know where I am. So just start walking south. It is getting to be dusk now. I come across a road where a lot of kids are partying, drinking beer and racing their cars. There are no houses and it is paved but a country road to be sure. So I try to buy a beer from someone. No one is willing to sell me or give me a beer. Now as I am walking along I see the RMCP pull up. So I hit the woods along the road and lay down to watch and see what is going on. The RMCP just tell the kids to keep it down and no more racing. The kids agree and the RMCP leave, so I come back out of the wood and continue trying to get a beer. No luck so I am about to surrender and continue upon my way when the RMCP reappear and this time tell the kids to pack it in and leave. So they are, all the cars are pulling out and roaring down the road. I stick my thumb out and a pick up pulls over and says get in back. So I do and off we go.

We get back into town and we pull over and one of the kids asks where I am going. I tell him I don't know I am trying to sneak back into America. He says why? So I tell him I just escaped from the RMCP and the Vancouver County jail but that I am wanted in the USA too. So I have to sneak back across the border and I don't know how. He says "Awesome! You're the Yank on the news. We are going to a few more parties and your welcome to come along then after we are done I will show you how to get back to the USA. My dad is a boarder guard so I can sneak you across."

I say "cool"

So we go to like 3 more teenager parties and drink beer and smoke pot. I tell my story at each party for entertainment. Then the kid takes me to the border and says "I am going to go in and talk to my dad and distract the other guards. You get out and walk into Peace Arch Park and keep heading into that direction toward the ocean. When you reach the ocean turn left and follow the ocean for about a half mile and you'll be in Blaine Washington. Good luck!"

Chapter Twenty Nine

I do as directed and I am back in the USA. I go to a little store and buy some pop. Then I go and make a collect call to my Lawyer Linda Mark in B.C. and tell her I am back in the USA so they can call off their dogs in B.C.

I stick out my thumb and catch a ride from a guy going to Seattle. I have him drop me off in Kirkland and I start looking for the address I know belongs to my wife's home. I find it after about an hour and go up to the door. Her roommate James is there but on his way out. So I go inside and am going to wait for her. While I am there I hit the answering machine to see if the cops have been asking around.

I don't really know how to use it so I back up the tape the whole way and just start listening. Well about the 3rd or 4th call I hear Sergeant Aerosmith. Annette answers the call after he identifies himself.

Sergeant Aerosmith says "Mrs. Thorson, do you know where your husband is?"

Annette Replies "Last I knew you people had him."

"No Ma'am, He Escaped last night, if he contacts you will you alert us?"

"Sure. Did he go into the woods?"

"We are not sure ma'am. But we believe so, if he didn't have any outside help" (implying she helped me or something by his tone of voice)

"Did he take a knife?"

"I don't know Ma'am I will have the kitchen do a count why do you ask?"

"Well you do know he was Special Forces and jungle trained. If he took a knife into the woods I wouldn't send anyone in after him unless you have a lot of body bags"

You can hear sergeant Aerosmith calling to another officer as he tries to cover the phone with his hand "Get the search squads back out of the woods and do it now." Then back to Annette "Ma'am, do you know what branch of the service he was in?"

"Air Borne Rangers, He was trained in Fort Poke. He was top of his class. Isn't this all in his records? Don't you know who you have there?"

"Yes Ma'am, but all it says in his records is Army Special Forces. No real facts are given so we would appreciate any information you could give us"

So Annette spent like 20 minutes making me appear to be a Rambo come to life. It was all bullshit, but she sure had the guard going for it and it was real fun to listen to. I wish I still had the tape but it got erased or lost.

So after listening to the tape I went to her cupboards and looked to see what I might find to eat. I found a bottle of Amoretto, so started drinking it. I went up stairs and looked out the bedroom window and saw my step-son Danny playing with some kids across the street. I stood there just taking it all in and enjoying the moment. Then I noticed a cop car pull in and park across the street from where the kids were playing. So I put the bottle down and grabbed my stuff, ran down stairs and out the door.

Now where Annette lived was an apartment complex that was built on a lot of keyhole cul-de-sacs. So I ran straight away from her apartment keeping the cop car between me and her corner apartment. Then when I was deep in the cul-de-sac, I turned and walked into view of the cop car acting like I didn't see him and didn't have a care in the world I headed towards the opening and only way out. As I was passing Annette's apartment again Danny was walking towards it. I was wearing my hat and sunglasses and red parka. I had to walk right past Danny and I knew if he recognized me the gig was up. But I looked at him and he looked at me and no flair of recognition. So I passed the test because I knew the cop would be watching closely. I turned down the road away from where the cop was parked and headed towards Juanita Drive.

I get down to where the fish house is across from Juanita Beach and try to buy something to eat with my Canadian money. No luck. So I make a collect call to my mom and tell her where I am. Then I go across the street to the park and wait. As I am sitting in the park I see 3 squad cars and a Van with the Channel 5 King News Logo on it rushing by where I am sitting in the direction of my wife's apartment. Seems I made a good decision to split when I did.

My mom shows up at the fish house and I walk over and tell her what I just saw. She orders us a meal and takes me over to my Aunt Chris' house in Georgetown. When we get there my Aunt is trying to give me all kinds of old clothes. I don't want any of it. Then she breaks out her sons ID. Dale Allen Gullison. He was killed in a car accident in 1980. He is 2 years younger than me but it is good ID. So we go down to DOL (Department of Licensing) and I apply for some state ID. When I show them that this is all I have. Birth certificate and SSN Card they say it isn't enough. So I say My Mom is right there she can prove who I am. They check her ID and she vouches for me. They take my picture and hand over my ID. So now I have ID again.

Then My Mom and Aunt Sylvia take me to My Aunt Sylvia's place out at SeaTac. It is a trailer court. But out of the way a nice little place as far as trailer courts go.

Well I am only there for about an hour and my brother Michael shows up. Says "Hey Bro. wanna go have a few drinks with me?"

"Sure Bro lets go" so we go to a little bar not too far away. We order a pitcher of beer and are flirting with this barmaid that must be 50 years old. But it is fun. After the second pitcher, a trio of good looking babes come in and sits in a booth all by themselves.

So I give Michael the nod and he looks and says "No they are waiting for someone." So I figure this is his bar so he knows.

After about 30 minutes no one shows up so I catch one of the girl's eyes and give them a nod, I get a nod of interest back and all of a sudden there is all kinds of whispering and talking behind their hands going on with a little giggling. So I tell Michael "Them girls are not waiting on anyone." I grab my glass and walk over and says "Hiya Ladies, how y'all doing tonight?"

They respond "Just fine."

"Do y'all mind if my brother and I join ya?"

"No there's plenty of room."

Right then Michael calls from across the room "I am leaving you can come now or your walking home."

I tell the Ladies "I'll be right back hang on ok?" and I run out to the parking lot to see what's up and tell Michael these girls are single and willing to let us join them. But he is set upon leaving. I should have let his dumbass leave and went back to the ladies, but I didn't have much money and I didn't want to be a bum. So I left the lovely ladies to hang with my brother.

We go back to the trailer court and over to my Cousin Shelly's place. She is an Amazon 6'2", 240 pounds and likes bar room brawling. So

Michael and I walk in together, side by side laughing and having a good time. Then he sucker punches me in the face. I reflex and punch him two quick rabbit punches and he ducks behind Shelly. She likes Michael so come to his defense standing between Michael and me, bellowing "You're not fighting in my house!"

So I reply "No problem" then turning to Michael I say "Come on boy why don't you and I step outside and finish this?"

Shelly is still bellowing about something and Michael is sitting down. He says "Nope, I ain't going outside tonight"

So I say "You can't stay in here forever boy. I will be waiting for you outside."

I go out and sit on his car. A few minutes later Shelly comes out bellowing on top of her lungs. "I said you're not fighting here so get away from my house."

Well this is a trailer court and folks do call cops around here so I leave and go back over to my Aunts trailer. As I walk in To Tall is at the door. Shelly is his kid sister.

So he roars, "You called my sister a bitch?!" and he stands right in front of me with his chest all puffed out.

"No I didn't To Tall shut up and sit down"

"Shelly just called me and told me you called her a bitch"

"I told you I didn't call her a bitch but if you don't get out of my face I might."

"Don't you ever call my sister a bitch!"

"Your sister is a Bitch!" and I punched him. He grabbed my parka and tried to pull it over my head. I just let it slip off as it was real loose anyways and started throwing sets on him backing him across the front room. Not trying to hurt him just backing him off me and letting him know I am not the one to try to push around. He stumbles over his girlfriend and her baby and falls on to the couch. Then the girl screams "Stop it before someone gets hurt. You almost hurt the baby!" So I stop and I tell To Tall "Look I am tired I am going to curl up on the floor over here and go to sleep. Don't come near me."

About 15 minutes later my Aunt Sylvia came home and To Tall starts in with his version of events. His Mom just says "To Tall take your girlfriend and go to bed." To me she says "Don't worry about it try to get some sleep." So I just roll over and go to sleep.

The next morning I call Annette and tell her I have to be somewhere else I can't stay here. So she sends Dipse, a friend of hers and Dipse's to pick me up. He is a Farwest taxi cab driver and works with David. So Dipse comes and gets me and takes me to Sherry's Restaurant on 116th Ave in Kirkland. David and Annette are there waiting for me. I decide to go to Montana. I have an old girlfriend there. So it is decided that David will take me as far as Spokane. David tells me that his town house and Annette's apartment are being watched. I tell him ok, like I thought he was over exaggerating the whole thing. But hey it is his story he can tell it anyway he wants.

David has his Taxi waiting outside in the parking lot. We eat and then get into the Taxi and are off, except, David wants to drive by Annette's apartment to show me the undercover car sitting down the block. He doesn't warn me he just does it. That makes me want to kill him on the spot. There is nothing like taking unnecessary risks with my freedom, so now I think we are off. But next thing I hear him say is "Now around this corner by my house is a white car 2 cops sitting in it." We drive right passed them and then he says "And up ahead look, another one." Man I am pissed and am letting him know it in no uncertain terms. All he has to say is, "Cops never pay too much attention to taxi cabs." It's just another case of 'Cops being just as stupid as you let them be'. But I still want to kick his damn ass. It wasn't as much fun for me as it was for him I guess.

The rest of the ride to Spokane is uneventful. David drops me off and gives me his wallet and forty bucks. The wallet is empty but it is a wallet.

I hitchhike into Billings Montana. Only takes a couple days. I go up to Verna's door, not knowing what my reception might be. It is a cool reception at first as I haven't contacted her since I escaped.

But she warms up and everything is cool by dinner time.

In the morning I start looking for a job Verna gives me her bank card. But I am having a hard time at first finding a job. But Verna finds one at a second hand store. Then I land one doing dry-cleaning. Verna doesn't have a car so I go to a garage sale and find a pink girl's ten-speed. I start riding it around town to the store and to work. The little kids in the neighborhood stop me and inform me I am riding a girl's bike. I ask them, "How can you tell?" So they explain to me about pink being a girl's color and see this bar? If it was a boy's bike it would have a bar across here. I thank them for pointing that out to me.

Then Verna finds a men's black ten-speed bike at the secondhand store and brings it home for me. The same kids stop me again and tell me now I am riding a proper bike. I again thank them for helping me out that way, cause no boy wants to get caught riding a girl's bike. It was cute the way them kids were looking out for me that way. Small town atmosphere, you have to love it.

Well after I was doing ok, I decided I should let my mom know where I was. So I called my cousin Deann in Kelowna and told her where I was and asked her to call my mom so she wouldn't worry. She asked what my address was and I told her my mom didn't need that but gave her the phone number and told her to give it to my mom. She said she would. We talked for about a half hour then I hung up. But for me to stick around incase my mom wants to talk to me. I say ok.

About two hours later there is a knock at the front door. I can see it is a Police Officer so I start to head out the back door. But there is standing another Police Officer with his gun drawn. So he walks me back in and Verna has already told the first Cop that Robert is here. But I am pulling out ID and claiming to not know where Robert is. He's not home right now and I don't know when to expect him back.

The cop says "Robert Thorson has a peacock tattooed on his left forearm. Would you mind pulling up your shirt sleeve?"

At this point I break and run. I make it barely to the street and I am tackled, having to open doors on the way out slowed me down too much. So I am busted.

Down at the station I notice on the warrant it says:

Crime Stoppers Alert from Kelowna B.C. Geraldine Thorson States "I don't know the address but if you can locate this phone number he is living there." If suspect is apprehended award Geraldine Thorson 1000.00 U.S dollars Per Crime Stopper awards system.

I call my Mom and tell her. She then tells me that it was Gerry that turned me in last time. I ask her why she didn't tell me? I was using her as a character witness in my Refugee Status case. She probably had something to do with me losing that too. Also had I known I wouldn't have called her to send a message to you. My mom says she didn't tell me because she didn't want me to hate my aunt.

A B.A.D. decision on my mom's part but I can see her reasoning. My mom knew I lived by a code where snitches died. The lesson I learned from this was "Even your family can betray you"

I didn't fight extradition. As I read the laws on escape before I escaped. Escape is always in the back of my mind so I was always reading the laws. At the time of my escape the law said only prior escapes would count against me and since they couldn't count the escape from Canada and I had plea bargained one of the other escapes away I only had one escape conviction. So the sentencing range was like 90 to 180 days for this escape. I thought this would also put me under the new guidelines and that would reduce my sentences and in a couple years I might actually get out. So to me it was a winning situation.

Chapter Thirty

Well when I get back, as luck would have it the law changed on July 1st, while I was on Escape. So now the Court can count all my prior convictions at sentencing. But they are supposed to count any sentences run concurrent as one point. So I would have like 3 or 4 points.

While I am in the county jail the gulf war kicks off with desert storm. So I write to the newspaper and state the law RCW. 900 that say in a time of war the state can send prisoners to war, so I tell them why don't they empty out the prisons and county jails instead of sending all those college kids over there. The prisons are where we as Americans keep out warrior class men. None of us are afraid to pull the trigger and if you offer us a clean slate with an honorable discharge. We will do whatever is left of our prison sentences in the military. That way the state doesn't have to support us. We can support ourselves and if we don't get an honorable discharge or mess up while in the Military you can always put us back in prison.

The argument that then we would be military trained outlaws doesn't wash because in prison are green berets, recon rangers, navy seals, airborne rangers and all kinds of martial artists. We share out knowledge with each other so most of us are already military trained, and if we get killed while over there fighting for our country? According to public opinion no great loss right?

The Vancouver paper printed part of my letter. I still think it is a good idea. The Law says 'Any one not convicted of treason, First degree murder or rape of a child may be inducted into the military during times of war.' Who better to fight our wars then warriors with something to gain? A second chance at a clean record is a powerful motivation for most. But it never happened. We are still sending fresh faced kids over there to die for their county.

We start preliminary hearing and they are bringing me plea bargains that say plead guilty and we will give you nothing but you will save the state money. I am saying no way. Give me second degree escape and I will cop to it. They say no.

So I tell them fine let's take it to trial.

My Lawyer says "What is your defense?"

"I didn't escape I was abducted by aliens" now in the Newspaper in Clark County Washington was an article about cattle mutilations. The Title of the article was 'Cattle Mutilations Aliens or Government Cover-up?' so I tell my lawyer about the article and that I am claiming I didn't escape I was abducted so it wasn't my fault.

He laughs out loud and says "Ok that's our defense?"

So now the DA is trying to get me take a plea bargain offering to recommend the lower range on the sentencing guidelines, if I don't cost the state a lot of money with a jury trial. But he still wants me to cop to first degree escape. But I say nope I want second degree escape or we go to jury trial. Because all I need is one person on the jury to buy my story and I walk scot free.

We go to jury trial. They bring the states witnesses and none of them actually saw me leave the prison grounds but none of them saw bright lights in the evening sky either.

I get up on the stand and explain about little grey men putting long needles in my belly button and show a scar on my arm where they took skin samples. I tell them about anal probes and how painful it all was with no pain killers. How I thought they were going to kill me. Then I woke up in a field and I didn't know I was in Canada. But when I found out I contacted my relatives and I was going to turn myself in but before I could there was an anonymous phone tip to the police and I was arrested.

The jury didn't buy it, but what the heck it was fun. The judge at sentencing time didn't see the humor in it.

He said "Mr. Thorson the sentencing range for your crime would be 18 to 24 for months. But since you saw fit to turn my Courtroom into a circus for your own amusement and since you seem to be a career criminal, I am going to count each of your priors as a point and sentence you to 38 months with 6 points. If you don't feel that is correct you can take it up on appeal."

So I got an exceptional sentence for my fun and the court of appeals like our countries whole justice system is a joke, but not a very funny one. So although I try my lawyer deserts me and I get the shaft. My new lawyer fights against me. He doesn't want the job so switches sides. Gets my case tossed out.

So I get sent to Shelton for processing. While I am there I am walking the yard. I notice a young Mexican standing beside the track and I give him a casual nod. Next time I come around he joins me and says "You think you know me?" I don't really remember him from anywhere but to be polite and to draw him out I say "You look a little familiar"

He says "I look like my Uncle Poncho. He is a tough guy in here isn't he?"

I say "Not so tough, I kicked his ass and knocked him out cold on the dining room floor."

"No you didn't!"

"Just be careful who you call a liar in here kid, those are fighting words to most folks and you don't want to try to climb this tree."

"Just wait until I tell Poncho what you said."

"Tell who ever you want to, but give me 30 feet for now"

I could tell this kid had illusions about who his uncle really was. I didn't want to have to smash him because of some misplaced loyalty on his part.

The next week I am shipped off to Walla Walla. I am put back into 8 Wing. Everything is going good. No job but Annette is sending money. I get put into a cell with a drug dealer named T.J. a good artist and we hit it off right away. So as a hustle we start drawing up greeting cards with art work on them and catchy little phrases to sell on store day for coffee and tobacco. We are doing a pretty good card business and drawing an occasional tattoo pattern. We both draw and have really different styles. Then we start moving kids in and tattooing them for money. We would move a kid in that had money and make him support the house or pay for his tattoos and then move him out when he had all the tattoos he wanted and move in another kid.

But with that come a lot of heat, the guards kicking in your house and taking your drawing and patterns.

After I am there for about two weeks I am out in the Big Yard on the phone talking to Annette and I see Poncho and his nephew walking up on me so I tell Annette to hang on I may be going into a fight so I have to put the phone down for a second. If someone else picks it up to just hang up as I will be on my way to the hole and will call her later. So I let the phone hang by the cord and turned to face the two Mexicans.

Poncho walks up like he wants a brotherly hug arms out stretched. I stop him by squaring off into a fighting stance as he get about 8 feet from me and say "What do you want?"

He says "No Thor, we are cool dude. I didn't know who you were back then." He puts his hand out for me to shake as a gesture of friendship. But if he gets control of my hand I am at a disadvantage in a fight with two to one odds.

So I tell him "I am not shaking your hand, the last time I saw you we were not on the best of terms. Now if you don't mind I am on the phone."

"Ok Thor we will talk to you later but as far as I am concerned we are cool and all that old shit is just so much water under the bridge."

"Ok, see ya later."

Well one day in the dining hall this big Indian named Psycho comes and takes the cookies off of my tray as he walks by.

I tell him "Go ahead and keep those cookies since you put your dick skinners on them but in the future ask before you take something off of my tray."

He says "Don't catch a bitch attitude on me" now Psycho is 6 foot and 250 pounds of solid muscle, so is used to people just bowing down to his will. I get up and light his ass up. I pop him in the mouth a few times before he even gets a swing off. But he is big and slow. I duck under his haymaker and jab him like 3 more times in the face before his next swing. If he connects I will be hurtin' for certain. But I am thrillin his big slow ass and he is making me look good because all he is hitting is thin air where I was. I love fights like this. You can watch him get set to throw a punch and have plenty of time to make him miss. But I am not doing him a lot of damage. I am hitting him solid but he is one healthy Indian. So finally the guards break it up and take us both to the hole.

When we get out T.J. tells me since I fought a skin in the circle I have to fight them all. I am cool with that. So I go to the Indian Wit man (Chief to you white boys). His name is Donnelly. I say "Rumor has it that since I fought one of you, I have to fight you all, how do you want to do that? One at a time or all of you together? Name your time and place and the conditions of the fight."

Donnelly says, "Your fucken crazy Thor, no one is going to bother you. Don't worry about it we like your style."

So I told my cellies to stand down no big deal. As they were willing to go to war with me if need be.

The next day I see ole Spike, I haven't seen Spike in years and I am happy to see him. So I say "Spike!" Spike recognizes me right off and Says "Thor, my friend how are you after all these years, you still look good."

I say "Spike I am doing just great, but I have to ask you something"

"Well what is it Thor, you can ask me anything"

"Spike, where were you on July 4th 1983?"

"1983? Why I just don't know Thor that was a long time ago. Why is this so important?"

"Well Spike, I'll tell ya, on July 4th 1983 you were in Monroe and you, dusty and I had just got done playing a game of handball, dusty and I against you, you had beaten us. So we were laying in the grass out front of the gym smoking a joint and you said "Dusty ten years from now I am going to ask you what you were doing on July 4th 1983, and you will say Spike I was in Monroe with you and Thor smoking a joint in front of the gym after you had beaten Thor and I at a game of handball" or something like that"

Spike brightens up and laughs out loud and says "I remember that I remember that! Wait until I find Dusty! I will remind him of that. Thank you Thor." I heard him retelling that story over and over for months to come.

This guy named Wilson moves into our cell. He seems pretty cool in for murder. He starts telling us he was a Recon Ranger in Vietnam and how he killed gooks with his bare hands. Tells us of some special ops he was on. So we are all delighted at his entertaining stories.

Well one night I grab my clamp lamp and flash it at T.J. and say in a German accent "Answer ze Questions"

Wilson says "Cut it out right now!" Well I ain't good at taking orders. If you tell me to sit you're forcing me to stand.

So I tell Wilson "Chill out dude we are just having a little fun."

He says "Don't make me kill you"

I say "Your Killer broke?"

He gets up. I am scared to death, I have heard his stories and I know he is a straight killer with his hands and feet. But I ain't going down without a fight and I ain't backing down. So he moves towards me and I unleash with everything I know. I have been trained by recon rangers, green berets and airborne rangers. I have been trained by the best the government has to offer plus a few martial artists along the way. Wilson folds and never gets a shot off. I smashed him with a quickness he won't soon forget. Never make your opponent so afraid of you that he is fighting for his life. Because if he thinks he might die, he has nothing to lose. He is fighting for his life with everything he has.

I smashed Wilson he never stood a chance. So after I see he is beaten I step back and tell him "Sit down on your bed and shut up mutherfucker this is my cell I make the rules."

Then I go sit at my desk and try to calm down. Wilson picks up a bic pen and says "With this pen I could kill you"

I grab two of my art pens with metal tips, one in each hand and say "Get to killing then mutherfucker!"

Wilson steps back by the front of the cell by the bars and starts loud capping (Yelling) "Are you pulling a weapon on me? Are you pulling a weapon on me?"

I tell him in a quiet steady voice "Why you yelling mutherfucker you want to draw attention? You need protection or something mutherfucker? You better drop that pen and shut the fuck up and get on your bed or start fighting!"

So he drops the pen and lies down on his back with his hands on his chest not saying a thing.

That night I sleep with one of my pens in my hand as I sleep right above Wilson in the same bunk beds. In a four man cell in Walla Walla there are two sets of bunk beds, but the cell does better with 3 felons. Four is just two crowded, even friends will fight if you over crowd them.

My other two cellies say "How did you sleep? We were awake all night expecting him to make a move during the night."

I tell them "I sleep light if he had made a move I would have killed him."

The next day Wilson leaves for work so I dig and pull his paperwork out of his foot locker.

He was in for murder alright. He was beating up his girlfriend when her 16 year old son and his friend came home. The boy said "Stop it, leave my mom alone or we will kick your ass old man" so Wilson did stop. The kids then went out in the backyard. Wilson came out a few minutes later and told the 16 year old. You were quite a man in there sticking up for your mom. I am proud of you and I want to shake your hand. The kid took Wilsons right hand and Wilson stabbed him to death with the knife he was holding in his left hand. Wilson was left handed.

So when Wilson came home from work I told him, baby killer you have to move and you have to move today. He went and told Sergeant Crow what I said. Crow came to the cell and told me they couldn't move him today but if I had a problem with him they could move me to the hole. So Wilson is a rat too, fucken punk. So I told Wilson as soon as Crow was gone to not move off his bunk while he lived here. He could use the bathroom but he was not to talk to anyone in this cell and not to move off his bunk or I would kick his ass. My cellies said "No! We will all kick your ass!"

The dead kid's mom still came to visit Wilson, she said because she loved him. How do you love a piece of shit that kills your son because your son stood up for you when the piece of shit was beating on you? I guess there are some things about women I will never understand.

Three days later he moved. But I told everyone his story. His younger brother was there. So I caught wind that they were both going to jump me. So I confronted them in the yard and told them "You're both pieces of shit and that Wilson my ex cellie was a rat and a baby killer. Now do something mutherfuckers." They both peed (Were too scared to do anything). Everyone saw it so they checked into 5 Wing (Protective Custody).

Now one morning, around June 1993 I didn't go to breakfast. I usually only went when it was hotcakes or french toast. Well, my other cellie Jay came back and says T.J. got his ass beat by The Beak. He says The Beak told T.J. to not sit in his seat anymore. Well that was T.J.s seat and had been for about a year now. The Beak had just come in from 6 Wing about a month ago. So when I go to chow I start taking T.J.s seat to hold it down for him when he gets out of the Hole. Well The Beak had broken T.J.s nose so they decided to separate the two. They put T.J. in 6 Wing and The Beak back in 8 Wing.

So The Beak come out of the hole and tried to sit at T.J.s table but I am there and so he sits next to me. I tell him move that seat is taken and you can't sit at this table. His 3 cellies sit at the next table.

So one of them says to me "Who the fuck do you think you are?"

I say "I am the one telling him he can't sit here anymore." I keep my voice low and even.

His cellie says "I am his cellie and I have Life and I say he can sit there"

"I don't care about your life sentence asshole, I came in here with a 5 year beef and now I have 3 life terms keep fucken with me and I might catch number four on you mutherfucker"

"We are all his cellies and we will all jump you!"

I look them all over slowly, up and down and then I stand up. (They probably thought I was giving up the seat, they probably thought they had won) then I say "Jump mutherfuckers you don't look like more than a warm up to me" in a cold low even voice.

They all just ducked their heads and didn't say a thing. So I told The Beak (he was called that because of his long pointed nose) get the hell off my table and don't come back. He picked up his tray and left.

I get back to my cell and am feeling real proud of my little grandstand play in the dining hall. So I start bragging to one of my cellies. He says "You dumbass they weren't as afraid of you as you think."

I say "They didn't jump did they?"

He says "No, but it wasn't because they were afraid of you."

"Oh yeah then what were they afraid of?"

"When you stood up about 16 Indians stood up behind you. They were outnumbered 5 to one".

From that point on, The Beak never tried to sit at my table again. Yep my table I took ownership of it. So T.J.s honor had been salvaged to my way of thinking. If you're not willing to fight all comers for what is yours it won't be yours for very long.

Well T.J. was gone and I never saw him again. But when he needed a place to parole to I gave him Annette's number and told him to call her and he could go there. What a little backstabber he turned out to be. Even before he was out Annette was visiting him, (She told me Walla Walla was too far to drive to visit me.) and then she wanted a divorce because she was going to marry T.J. so I filed for it and let her go. I mean I have seen guys threaten the girls to try to make them stay, but why? You can't force them to stay for long and there are plenty of little convict groupies (girls that go from one convict to another) that will take their place. So let them go and get another one. Convicts ain't to picky, so all the little fat girls that can't find a guy on the streets can find a man that is a little dangerous and will profess his undying love for them, tell them they are beautiful and they know where he is and that he isn't cheating on them, as long as they keep visiting and putting money on his books. That is all good until he gets out and kicks them to the curb for a drug bag or another woman.

Chapter Thirty One

So my next new cellie is Martin, and he is trying to make a cassette tape letter home to his girlfriend Jane. But he can't think of anything to say. So I start teasing him about the tenth time he said "Umm" he started to shut the tape off as we were supposed to be quiet while he did this. But I told him leave it on and introduce me to your lovely babe. So he did and I then I gave a little back ground on myself and Martin and I bantered with Martin and had fun making the tape for his ole lady. As it turned out it, it was a real funny tape.

Well in about 4 days when the mail is delivered I get a card with 40.00 bucks in it from some girl named Judy. She says she is a friend of Jane's and heard the tape, and would I call her?

Hell yeah, I will call her. She has already won my heart she sent me money. I am a cheap man whore; the way to win my heart is give me money.

So I start calling Judy and she wants to come and visit me. So I send her a visiting form so her and Jane can make the long ride from Stanwood to Walla Walla.

Now about the second visit or so I find out Judy is married to John. Now I really don't care if she is married. But she has John bringing her up and John is sending me money, and that's weird. So I ask her what is up with all this? Is she leaving John or just playing around? Because facts are I don't really care I just want to know what is going on in her head.

She says she doesn't know. So I got it figured she is just playing the field in a safe way with a bad boy.

Well Judy and Jane start a writing campaign to get Martin and I moved to Monroe where it would be closer to visit. But Martin in so short (has very little time left) they just send him to camp. But in October 1993 the letter writing worked and I am transferred to Monroe (W.S.R.)

I land a really good job in the print shop thanks to one of my good pals Tilly. It pays good wages $1.10 an hour. Starts at .35 cents an hour but Tilly has an in, so I jump to $1.10 the following month. I work with Tilly in the Tab shop making tabs for cars for about 3 months then transfer to the bindery.

There the state is losing money because a lot of jobs are sent out all messed up and are coming back to be redone. Now we did a lot of work for the state and state agencies like Fire Departments and Police Departments as well as the legislators and the Department of Corrections. So they wanted their documents and business cards to be nice.

So the first thing I did with the knowledge I gained from working with Tilly was to start making the guys do it right. I told them I was not going to send anything out that was not up to par and if it made it to me they would have to redo it.

Now understand these were Inmates mostly not real Convicts. Most of the Convicts were all gone by this time. So most of these guys were getting paid low wages and complaining to the boss about each other. I put an end to that. I told them I wanted good products and if there was any problem with typesetting or paper supply to come to me first and I would get them what they needed. Then if I didn't get what I wanted (their best effort) there would be problems.

The first thing I found was a pressman would burn a plate with bad typesetting when he knew it was bad because he didn't care. Then he would complain he couldn't fix it because he had wasted all the paper for that run. The paper room guy would tell the boss if they asked for more paper and they might get fired.

The type setters didn't care what the typeset looked like as long as they could smoke pot in the darkroom. That was the important thing about working in typesetting. You could smoke pot while you worked.

Well I told them if the type setting didn't come out right for my pressmen to turn out a good product for me to ship I was kicking someone's ass in that darkroom.

Amazing the type setting improved 100% and these press operators knew what they were doing. Pretty soon they were competing with each other for whom could do a job the best.

The guy in the paper room was still telling the boss, but he was telling the boss Louie that I made him give me paper under threat of kicking his ass or I would just walk in and take what I wanted with no thought to his inventory slip.

After about 3 months Louie calls me to his office. He is tired of this guy complaining to him about me stealing paper.

So Louie says "Thor I have it on good authority your stealing paper"

I ignored that accusation, and asked "Hey boss how is business? Are we still losing money or are we making money? How many orders did we get back this month?"

Louie says "Hey on that note, business is good and we are doing much better. I don't think more than 3 orders were returned this month and we are finally making money."

I say "Great. Now the reason for that is, I run this shop. I see to it that nothing goes out that doesn't meet my approval. So I want all the guys in the shop to be paid 1.10 an hour (Which is the most you can get paid for that position)

Louie says "No way I can't do it and why should I?"

I say "Because the reason all the stuff goes out all messed up every day is we are always training new guys, and they don't know what they are doing. If we pay well from the start the guys that know what they are doing won't change jobs. Then we will get consistent work out of them, and I will see to it that nothing messed up goes out. Because if it is messed up I will know it wasn't an accident. Then I will take care of it."

"I still can't pay 1.10 an hour to everyone."

"OK fine I quit you can go back to the shit you were doing before I showed up"

"Wait, what if I give them 35 cents the first month and a dime raise a month?"

"Forget it I am out of here."

"Ok, what if I give them 35 cents the first month and then raise them to 90 cents the next month and a nickel a month after that until they reach 1.10? They will reach 1.10 in 6 months."

"Ok, it's a deal."

"What do you want me to do?"

"Nothing, stay in your office and I will fix everything I can, if I can't fix it I will come let you know."

"But what am I to do while I am here?"

"Nothing, just stay off the floor, I will handle everything. You will get paid to sit and play on the computer."

"Ok"

Now about this time the 'Three Strikes You're Out Law' came into effect so the Everett Herald Newspaper come to the prison and asks to interview a couple felons on how they think it will affect the prison population. So the Warden (Superintentdent) calls me out for the Convict Opinion and a Black Guy named Andre for the Inmate Opinion, and of course Andre is sure it is a conspiracy to keep the black man down and it will mostly only affect the black population etc.

I tell them that if you lock a guy up and take away his hope. He has nothing to lose and with nothing to lose everything is gain. So, if I have forever, I have no hope of good time or ever being released and one of these pencil neck small minded guards on a power trip gets in my face, what's to stop me from slicing him belly button to collarbone? Or popping out one of his eyes and eating it like a grape while he watches with his other eye? Or just beating his ass? Are you going to give me 20 more years on top of forever? As long as I don't kill the guard there is nothing you can do to me. Are you going to lock me in a cell? I already live in a cell. So the hole is just another cell with room service and it is a single man cell. As crowded as the prisons are getting a single man cell is a luxury.

Then when I am too old to fight anymore, you the tax payer will be paying for my medications and health care. So since I won't be able to be housed with younger more dangerous felons anymore you will have to start building prisons for the aging felons that you gave forever. At that point you can't turn them loose because they won't know how to live in society. I almost didn't know how to adapt after 27 years. They are already building senior homes for prisoners in Washington State as of 2008. But the paper edited what I said and misquoted me and left out most of what I thought was the good parts. But they gave me front page coverage and pissed off a lot of guards.

This one guard I don't remember his name. But he kept smarting off to me and making little disrespectful comments and noises whenever I walked by him.

So after like the third day I stopped in front of him and said "You got a fucken problem with me Mutherfucker? If so why don't you find an empty cell you and I can step into and I will solve your fucken problem for you real quick or you can shut the fuck up when I walk by. Ok?" he didn't say a thing he just ducked his head in fear. From that point on when I walked past him and looked him in the eye he ducked his head and looked at the ground. He was bigger than I was, he just didn't have any heart.

Well around this time Judy decided she wanted to get married. The prison had a conjugal visit program but they were changing the rules. After June 1st if you were not married prior to coming to prison you wouldn't be able to get married and get conjugal visits. So if we wanted to get them Bone Yard visits we had to get on the stick.

No Judy wasn't about to divorce John he was her meal ticket. So we would just have to work around that. She forged some divorce papers that passed the administrations' review and we got married.

Life was good Judy had two husbands still does to this day in fact I never divorced her and she started the divorce proceedings but never followed through. I was fighting them because since I was married if I could find a babe to change her name legally in a court to Judy's name when I wasn't at Monroe I could still get bone yard visits. But I am getting ahead of myself now. So now since John either didn't know or didn't want to know, we had to find ways for her to visit for 3 days at a time.

PRISON STORIES FROM GLADIATOR SCHOOL

Well I have been a Wiccan Priest since 1977 mostly just to be able to get things like incense and other things the prison doesn't normally allow felons to have. But I never had anyone on the outside willing to help me do stuff. Judy Founded The Circle of Magic. So now we were having group meetings and casting the circle, raising a cone of power. But it gave Judy an excuse to tell John she was going to a Wiccan retreat once a month and it was an all female thing so he wasn't welcome. She was spending those three days at Monroe with me. So I was having a real good time at Monroe. We had fasts for 24 hours then the prison was supplying a feast in the form of a big bag of food for us to take back to our cells and consume after midnight. I was buying incense 1000 sticks at a time and doling them out to felons that couldn't afford to buy it and I was buying books 5 at a time same title so we could study. Plus at the print shop I was taking more expensive lesson books and cutting the binding off and making 40 copies at a time and putting spiral bindings on them because they work better for a lesson book.

I used to go out to the gym quite a bit and they had this really cute little blonde working out there named CO McGee. So I would flirt with her as would a lot of guys. But I always kept it clean and just in good fun.

One day I get called to the Control Booth and am told to report out to the gym. It is about 7:30PM and the gym closes at 8:00PM. So I get out there and I say with a big smile "What's Up?" Because, Ms. McGee has become my friend at this point, and I figure she needs a man to move something or some such nonsense.

But much to my surprise she says "Will you stay with me while I close up?"

Now I am thinking she likes me and wants to do something behind closed doors. So I says "Sure" I mean she is absolutely beautiful and sweet. I have heard about guys doing it with guards before and I had a couple opportunities myself but always let them go before. But Ms.

McGee I am half in Love with anyways. So we hang out walking around together and chatting as the gym clears out. Then she says "Let's just do a sweep to be sure everyone is gone."

I say "Ok'

So we do and she walks me back up to the exit and says "thanks a lot Thor you can go now."

Again I am shocked. So I say "Why was I here?"

"I have been getting threatening letters about someone wanting to rape me"

Now where she is posted she is definitely in danger of that. So I tell her I will be here every night from now on.

As I am leaving I am called to the sergeant's office and CO Best. The Coolest Guard in the joint is waiting for me. He says Ms. McGee has been receiving threatening letter and would I look out for her while he does the investigation to find out who is stalking her. I tell him I have already told Ms. McGee I would be there for her and that I would also starting seeking who is doing this to her. He says "You'll tell me what you find out?"

"Not on a bet. But I will solve the problem".

He says "No Thor, not that way it has to be done right"

"Well then you better hope you find him before I do"

CO Best did. He found him the next morning while I was at work and before Ms. McGee came to work. So CO Best is a hero he saved a rape-os life.

Chapter Thirty Two

Well meanwhile out at the print shop Jimmy worked in the typesetting room with Chuck and Buddy.

So one day Chuck and Buddy come to me and ask "How thick do you think the floor is?"

I say "4 inches"

Buddy says "Then it has a solid metal plate under that."

I say "No it doesn't it's just concrete"

Buddy produces a magnet on a string and shows us it sticks to the floor. Then says "See, I have tested the floor everywhere"

I tell him "A solid sheet of steel would cost millions and even banks only do that under the safe. Not the whole floor because it would just cost too much and the state is not spending that kind of money on a warehouse."

Now this new industries building we worked in was outside the walls with a door through the prison parameter wall to reach it.

So I take the felons to where some pipes are going through the floor and show them that there is a finishing layer of black concrete on top or the rest of the concrete and we chip a chunk of the top finish off. Then try to stick the magnet to the bare spot and it doesn't stick anymore. But it will pick up the chunk we broke off.

But by this time I already know what is in the making. So I invite myself into the plan by saying "What's the plan, a tunnel?"

Buddy pipes up with "Yep" just as Chuck says "Nope" by then it was too late and I was involved.

So I ask where and Buddy says the darkroom in type setting. At this point Chunk walks away more than a little pissed.

Then I see Jimmy and Chuck coming back as Buddy and I conspire in the corner. But Jimmy is more than pleased that I invited myself along. He says he had considered weather to invite me before but hadn't known how to approach me.

So now I am taken to the dark room and shown what they got done so far which isn't a lot. He shows me an aerial photograph of the prison taken after the new Industries building was built. He got it from Louie, who got it from the Superintendent who wanted it blown up to go in a frame on his wall in his office. So he gives us the negative and says blow it up three foot by six foot in full color.

Well hell we wanted to blow it up anyways. So we just made an extra copy and cut it into 8½ by 11 sheets and kept it well hidden. It shows all the guard towers and the other prisons and their towers on the Monroe Prison Command grounds.

We get a 4 ton bottle jack from auto mechanics and bring it back to the darkroom in a plastic bag in the bottom of a mop bucket covered with water and suds. But the hole isn't big enough so we get a chisel and a hammer and knock the hole a little bigger so we can get the jack in there and we start breaking out little chunks until it is big enough for Chuck's fat ass to fit through.

I tell Jimmy and Chuck that they need to get into shape. So they start running every day after dinner and getting prepared. We start digging the sand out with a plastic water pitcher.But "Where are we going to get rid of the sand?" Jimmy asks me and I think on it. As bringing it out to the yard like in the movies isn't going to work for us, and tossing it in the garbage is going to cause suspicion. So since all the walls are sheet rocked I tell Jimmy can't we put it in the walls between the sheet rock? So that's what we do. We cut out a 6 inch by 16 inch wide piece of sheetrock near the ceiling and pull out all the insulation we can. Toss that in the garbage in tied off bags and fill the walls with sand and rocks. We have a bullet proof darkroom. Now someone must always be in the darkroom to alert the digger if a guard or staff shows up.

About this time the print shop is doing so well they have hired a second boss. Mr. Munsen, now Munsen thinking he is going to fix how we do stuff keeps coming into my bindery area. But he is working here because his printing shop went belly up. So one day he came into my area and starts telling me how to do stuff. He says I can't do things like I have been doing them. So I tell him "Why not?"

He says "Well, that's not how things are done on the streets."

I reply "I never seen the streets and ain't even sure they exist. But even if they do, this is not the streets this is prison and this *is* how we do things here."

He says "Well that's going to change now that I am here."

I reply "Dude, get the hell out of my area I have work to do and your just in my way."

He leaves, but my words must have been eating on his small mind because in 20 minutes he is back.

So I tell him "Are you lost?"

Munsen says "No. why?"

"Because you are my area again, why don't you go sit in your office and get the hell out of the way. *Men* are trying to work here."

"That's it, come with me to Louie's office" so I follow Munsen to Louie's office and he starts ranting and raving about me being disrespectful to staff.

Louie looks at me and asks what happened. I tell him Mr. Munsen is coming over in my area and trying to change rules I have established and just generally making a pest of himself I need him out of my area. Can't he go bother someone else?

Louie says "Mr. Munsen stay out of Thor's area."

So while we are digging the tunnel, we have one guy out in the typesetting spot, his job is to whistle when anyone comes in. Munsen wants to know why we do that and Jimmy tells him because we need to know if you are going to open a door when we are developing film. But Munsen goes back into the darkroom and sees a chess set with a game in progress. He says "Developing my ass it is to cover your chess game."

So we admit to it. Yep you caught us. He says "No problem I don't mind you guys playing chess."

So from that point on when he came into the type setter's room he would whistle to alert the digger he was there.

He was such a dumbass. He told me he was Norwegian. But I told him the SEN in his last name marked him as a Scandinavian. He tried to tell me no, the SON in a last name was Scandinavian. So I told him Dude I been teaching Asatru since 1977 and can tell him the whole history and all the legends' of the Gods.

He says "You know all the myths?"

I respond "They aren't myths to me and I would appreciate it if you didn't refer to my religion in such an unprofessional manner"

"You can't really believe in all those myths can you?"

"You're getting real close to a religious harassment suit buddy. Maybe you better go read the policy or ask Louie before you push this issue any farther"

So pretty much I am just messing with him but he is such a dickhead it's hard not to try to make his life as miserable as I can.

One day I am called for my opinion on something in the tunnel. As we are going under the foundation there is a red brick pipe running along the bottom of the cement foundation and the guys want to know do I think we should break it or dig under it? I vote for digging under it. I don't know what it is but don't want to chance it is sewer or something. They break it and plug both ends with plastic bags full of sand. It was the drain pipe for the roof.

So in late September we have the tunnel all dug. We are about a foot from the surface outside the wall. We use a metal rod to push up through the dirt so we know when it moves freely we are close. Then we take a piece of plywood and a 2x4 to shore it up, so it doesn't cave in prematurely. We have guard's coverall uniforms stolen from the dry-cleaning shop. We are ready to go with the first roll of fog in October. Well the fog comes and the fog goes. My partners are afraid to take the plunge. They have smuggled a lot of their property out and into the tunnel. In fact they dug a room beside the tunnel to store their stuff. I only have a sweat suit down there, nothing that has my name or number on it. But these guys who have never escaped before and have nothing except what they own here in the joint, want to take their radios and things with them. Dumbass move but I don't plan on staying with them anyways, as soon as we are clear of the prison grounds I am splitting to go my own way.

So October comes and goes. Plenty of fog but my partners are paranoid and I would have to fight them to get to the tunnel if I wanted to go alone. Because once the tunnel is opened on the other end there is no way to reclose it. So November comes and goes not as much fog as October but they want to wait for more fog.

December comes and goes almost no fog. Pretty soon we are going to have to go without fog. But it is starting to be dark when we go to work but I am beginning to realize no one is ever going to use the tunnel. These guys are caught up in the thought of how cool it is to have a tunnel that they could use.

So January rolls around and the rains come. Well the roof of this new building is flooding so the contractors are called back out to see why. They start by walking around the parameter with a heavy pole they are throwing at the ground looking for a soft spot where the water might be gathering. When they throw it at the top of our tunnel the heavy steel shaft just disappears into the ground. So they bring a back hoe, but at soon as the bucket of the backhoe touched the top of our tunnel the whole last bit of earth caved in.

So everyone that worked in the print shop was tossed in the hole, and the investigation began.

Now Jimmy, Chuck and Buddy all had things down there that had their DOC Number on it. No one else knew about it so no one was talking so everyone but the four of us were released.

The three of them are busted because of their own stupidity. I am busted because there are four guard uniforms. They said that even if I wasn't going, they felt sure I was involved in an advisory capacity if nothing else. They can't prove I was involved but, they don't need proof in the joint so they just find you guilty of something. I never got charged or infracted for it, but I got shipped off to Walla Walla again just the same.

Chapter Thirty Three

No big deal I am pretty Infamous by now. My hair is down to my waist and people that don't even know me know who I am say hi in passing hoping to be associated with me.

When I get there I am sent before a gang assessment squad. They want to know if I belong to the biker club or and a skin head or I am a peckerwood. I tell them I don't belong to any clubs. They ask "Not even The Woodpile?"

"What is that?"

They say "The racist white club"

"No. I don't belong but I know some like Parry. They come to the Odinist religious ceremonies." I have been teaching Norse Wicca and or Odinism since 1977 actually.

They say "No. Perry is a skinhead"

"Well then I really don't know what you're talking about."

So they let me go. It seems that since the last time I was here someone decided to start a chapter of the AB (Aryan Brotherhood) up here in the Washington prisons. Mostly in my opinion they were a disorganized bunch of dumbasses.

They would get the young white kids off the chain lure them in with a lot of tough talk about being down for the cause, White Power and all that bullshit. Send them out of missions to beat up someone and then not back them up.

They could have been a force to be reckoned with, if they tried but maybe they just were to stupid to run a tight organization. The guys at the top of the club were all afraid to fight their own battles and sent out kids to do their dirty work.

So I told the head of this little club that they could not recruit out of my cell as I am an Odinist and if any one lives in my house they are under my protection. So if anything bad happened to them I would be seeking the person responsible for sending my ward on a mission. Meaning I was coming for the woodpiles head members. A dumbass named Eightball who thought he was tough said "Thor you're too old to fight".

I said "Don't let 10 seconds of stupidity fuck off the rest of your life. Not you and 3 of your best warriors can take me down, and if you send someone after me because you're afraid to come yourself, don't disrespect me by sending some kids. Send real warriors, then when I and done with your front line I will be coming for you". Eightball shut up and never spoke to me again. But none of the kids in my house were recruited and if they joined my religious group they were not used for missions. A man's word is all he has in the joint and my word was good.

I had a lot of skinheads join my group but I told them it was not a white power group. They said they knew but it was a European group so only whites could join. Well one of our Gods created all the races, Heimdal son of Odin right? They would agree, and he created the races for a purpose. The fact that the whites planted their European seed in Africans is irrelevant. But now those Africans were half European so had as much right in this group as anyone else. If they argued still I would ask them what European tribe they belonged to. Norwegian, German or what? Then I would ask on their mom's side or their dad's? Then what was the other parent? Oh so you only claim your German side? Well why can't a black claim only his white side? They didn't like it and no blacks at Walla Walla ever tried to join the group. But I wanted it understood I would not hate the blacks or any minority just because they are a minority. I tend to hate people for their actions not their color. But being a white American, I do hate the coddling the minorities get. But that's our government at work not the minority's fault.

So things went pretty smoothly for the next couple years until I got sent out to medium custody, and the CUS and my counselor didn't want me there. They said with my escape history and infraction history I didn't belong out there. Then they said "If Marsh wasn't out here you would have more infractions they anyone in the joint."

So I said "How does Marsh has more infractions then I do? How many more?

"Not a lot he only has you by 3 Major infractions"

But that wasn't a fair comparison as they didn't count any infractions from before the computers were installed in the prisons to keep track of that. I had 10 years more in the joint that weren't counted, and Marsh didn't start his time until 1985. Computers came in around the same time as Marsh did. But I was about to break Marsh's record and gain a substantial lead on him.

About two months later I ran into a black correctional officer who came from the Deep South, CO Rippy.

Now Rippy was as racist as a guard can come and mouthy like a lot of blacks can be. So he would let the black folks slide on some things and write up the whites for the same exact thing he let a black brother go for.

So CO Rippy kept trying to get me to do little extra chores for him, which I refused to do. So he confronted me and said "Boy When I tell you to do something I want you to jump to it."

I said "Say Boy, you wasn't acting that way down south, in fact you weren't even looking white folks in the eye, so don't start getting all uppity with me now that we are up north."

Well CO Rippy was mad clear through but he just turned and walked away. A few minutes later I hear over the Intercom "Thorson report to the Sergeants Office"

So I go to see what all the fuss is about, and Sergeant Bowman and CO Rippy are in the office. The Sergeant is behind the desk. I come in a plop down in the chair across the desk from the sergeant.

Sergeant Bowman says "Thorson what is this racist bullshit you're pulling?"

I look around and say "The only racist in this office is CO Rippy. He has been trying to throw his weight around with the whites and letting the blacks get away with all kinds of shit and I am fed up with it."

"Well what did you say about him looking white men in the eyes?"

"I just told him when he was back in the south where we both come from, he wasn't looking white people in the eyes never mind bossing them around and he knows it's true. So I told him to quit acting so uppity just because he was up here in the north"

CO Rippy was standing in the only door way out of the room. I should tell you I am a little claustrophobic. I tend to panic when I feel trapped and will go into fight or flight mode. Only I don't do flight very well.

So at this point Sergeant Bowman gets up from behind his desk handcuffs in hand and starts moving towards me and CO Rippy starts to move towards me. I explode out of my chair into a fighting stance.

Both CO Rippy and Sergeant Bowmen clear the office. Then Bowman comes back and says "Are you alright?"

I say "Yeah just don't trap me or I will panic"

"Ok, just go lock up Thorson"

"Ok" and I go back to my cage and start packing as I am sure the goon squad is coming for me.

Nope. They never come. The next day CO Rippy comes and tells me to do some extra work duty for him. I tell him "Kiss my ass."

He says "If you don't do it I will infract you."

I tell him "So what punk just do your job don't tell me about it. In fact why don't you just write up a whole stack of them and don't date them that way it will be easier on you. Every day you don't even have to ask me just date one and put it in because I will never do anything you ask me to boy."

So every day for a month this punk correctional officers writes me a major infraction, and the punk hearing officer finds me guilty of them all and takes my custody than my yard for 18 months, my library for 12 months, my gym for 18 months and my personal clothing for a year. I never ever heard of a sanction like that. But I didn't really care either I didn't have a lot of clothes anyways. So then they take me back inside to 8 wing and closed custody.

But now I have 3 cellies and in a 4 man cell it is customary for 3 cellies to leave and one to stay back for some personal time and we rotate who is staying back. Men in cages without women need a little time alone occasionally. But with my sanctions I would not be allowed to leave the cell except for meals for about a year and a half. Well that wouldn't go over to well with my cellies I am sure. So I just started going to yard and gym and where ever I wanted to and the dumb correctional officers never noticed. Another case of correctional officers are as dumb as you let them be.

Well about a month later some dumb white kid beat up a Mexicans fag and continued to kick the fag after he was down. So the Mexican wanted to beat up the white kid and show him what it felt like to be defenseless and stomped out. But the white kid was positive cash flow to The Woodpile. He was bringing in a lot of pot. So The Woodpile said the Mexican could fight the kid but not stomp him out. But everyone knew the Mexicans weren't happy about that.

So when the day came that the fight was arranged on all the solid whites and all the Mexicans (Who are all solid) went to the big yard.

The Mexican and the white kid face off and the Mexican knocks the kid out in about 3 punches. Up to that point everything was fine, and true to his word the Mexican didn't put the boots to the kid but he bent over and continued to punch the kid in the head after he was down. We (The Whites) had the Mexicans outnumbered 3 to 1 easy. So when the Solid Whites rushed in (The weak whites ran and lined up against the wall to stay out of it) we were outnumbered 2 to 1. It was a sad day for American White Pride. I finished my Mexican quickly with a kick to the nuts and looked around. Then I saw Jamie a solid but skinny bi-polar kid had 4 Mexicans on him and he was swinging wildly. So I ran to his aid and kidney kicked two Mexicans from behind and they went down like timber, the other two saw what happened and ran. Jamie with his eyes closed is still wind milling his arms and runs into me so I catch his arms and say "Not me son" so Jamie opens his eyes. We look for our next target and about that time the correctional officers start shooting into the yard with live rounds. I grab Jamie and take him to the ground and tell him don't move and stay here.

Now at this point I didn't realize that more than half of the whites ran from the fight because I was too busy fighting and trying to stay alive to pay attention to what was going on with everyone else.

So the correctional officers come and used zip ties to handcuff everyone in the big yard. Then they take us all to the hole. It is at this point that one of the correctional officers says to me "Thorson what are you doing out here your on cell confinement."

I reply, "I am white, where did you expect me to be."

So we all go to the hole. Three days later I go up for my infraction.

I was infracted for refusing a sanction, assault and gang activity. The hearing Officer Lt. Lipski says "How do you plead?"

"Not guilty"

"Thorson we have you on video tape"

"Well, then why are you asking me?"

"The tape isn't very clear."

"Well then like I said I am not guilty"

"What about the refusing a sanction are you not guilty of that too?"

"Well that's a dumb question I was in the big yard so of course I am guilty of that but not guilty of anything else.

"Ok. Well I am finding you guilty on counts one, two and three."

"Well what did you ask me for if you weren't going to believe me anyways?"

Shut up Thorson, I am sentencing you to 10 days in Seg and an additional 30 days cell confinement. Do you want to appeal?"

"Of course, anything to give you guys a little more job security."

So after my 10 days they let me out of the hole.

Now Jamie who was released after 3 days has been telling everyone how he was surrounded by 8 Mexicans and going down when he saw me fighting my way to his side. I crossed the length of the big yard and was knocking Mexicans out as I came. I must have put down 10 or 15 Mexicans before I got to him and then I waded in and smashed another 6 before the last two had the sense to run. Then I pulled him down and shielded his body from gun fire.

Well folks I am here to tell you that is not what happened. But do you remember the cowards that stood against the wall? One of them named Bear says he saw it too or at least the end of it. So now I am bigger than life and bulletproof. I try denying it to anyone that will listen and tell them look Jamie is not right in the head. That didn't happen. But since Jamie has co-signers (Witnesses) my version of events is treated like I was down playing my part. Now yes it is true I did teach martial arts in my cell but I am not Bruce Lee by any stretch of the imagination.

Then is when I find out a lot of white boys didn't join the battle. I confronted the one named Bear and he said he had kids on the streets and had to think of them so couldn't help us out. So I told him I also have two kids on the street but right now I have to worry about my brothers in here. So I told him he was a weak pussy and to never talk to me again then I stood up in the dining hall and announced to the dining room at large. "If you sat against the wall during the Mexican white riot don't ever talk to me again because I will smash you if you do."

So I head out to the yard. When I get to the gate where the correctional officers are patting folks down before letting them into the big yard, one of the correctional officers says "Thorson what are you doing here?

"Going to yard."

"You have like 2 years loss of yard you can't go in here. You need to try to follow the rules."

"I don't need to try anything. I am going to do whatever I want whenever I want and if it so happens to coincide with your rules fine, but if it doesn't I don't give a fuck"

"Well go stand over there until we are done and I will escort you to the hole again."

He did and I got another 10 days in the hole for refusing a sanction. But while I was down there I noticed I was getting yard for an hour a day and was able to use the phone while at yard. Plus a single man cell is nice after living with two or three other personalities for any length of time, now these cells are a lot smaller only being 6 by 8 foot. So when my 10 days were up they told me "Alright Thorson your released back to 8-wing."

I said "Naw, I am cool right here."

"No. Thorson your released you have to go"

"Nope, go get the extraction squad because I ain't going anywhere."

"Why not?"

"Because in here I get yard and can use the phone and I get room service."

"Fine, stay then I don't care."

Because if I have to fight the Goon Squad they have to put me back in here anyways so they couldn't win. Poor bastards probably never been in that situation before and didn't know how to act. Most guys are more than happy to get out of the hole.

So they slam the door and wait about 10 days and come back and tell me again. "Thorson your released to 8-wing"

"Nope, I ain't going, I am cool right here"

They say "Thorson you have to go we need the cell".

I reply "So. That's your problem not mine."

"Thorson if you don't come out of that cell we will send you to IMU" (IMU is the Supermax Isolation Building)

I say jokingly "Are you threatening me with a window and a TV?"

"Thorson we are not joking "

"You are! You're threatening me with a window and a TV" and I laugh at them. Now the cell I am in is a 6 by 8 foot cell. The cells in IMU are 8 by 12 and have a window that can't open it is about 3 foot tall and 6 inches wide. But it is a window, then after a month they give you a color TV with cable and again it is a single man cell. By this point in my life I have become antisocial anyways and just like to read and workout. Well the cell is big enough to work out in and I get a shower every day. It has air-conditioning and central heating. So I like it out there. I don't have to put up with no one else. My clothes are a pair of coveralls and the state washes them weekly for me. What's not to like?

So I refuse the housing assignment and they ship me out to IMU within a week. But before I go I am trying to get other felons to refuse to leave the hole to just to mess with the Administration. But no other felons are with me on this, so I take this road high alone.

Chapter Thirty Four

I get out to IMU and they put me in a cell right next to Bulldog. He is a solid white boy from Oklahoma. He sends me a care package of toothpaste and some coffee. Bulldog is never getting out. Troll is on the other side of Bulldog so the three of us spend our time telling war stories and working out. I tell Bulldog about the ab program I have and he says it is a sissy program. I just agree with him. After all I have a six-pack and he has a little round fat keg. But a couple days later I hear him telling Troll how he tried my program and his gut was all fucked up. So then he has Troll doing it with him. I on the other hand don't work out just an hour or two a day I am working out all day. 800 pushups in 10 sets of 80 each, I am doing tricep extensions from the sink, jumping jacks, back arms from the bed, stretches, chin ups from the shelf and Katas. But even after my 800 normal pushups I do extras with my feet up on the bed and my hands on the floor and hand stand pushups too. Just to work the muscles a little differently. But pretty much with nothing else to do I would get up and work out any time my pump went down. ('Pump' is the swelling in your muscles when they fill with blood from working out). So to me life was good. Because all I am working for in the pump. All my needs were taken care of and I had the time to work out all day.

Well six months go by and I go to a hearing to see if I can get a better custody and get out of IMU. They are willing to release me no problem as I haven't really done anything to be here.

So I ask "If I go out do I have to finish the sanctions I had before I came in here?

They reply "Yes, the sanctions will still be in effect."

So I say "I ain't going anywhere, see ya in another year."

"Mr. Thorson. That isn't your decision to make. We haven't made a decision yet. But be prepared to be released in the next few days."

So I get back to my cell and I tell the felons what happened. They want to know what I am going to do so I let them know I ain't going anywhere until the sanctions are dropped. They understand.

What I am doing is the solid thing to do. As no one likes to have a cellie that just won't leave the house. Everyone needs some time alone.

Well in 3 or 4 days sure enough, the CO in the booth says "Thorson, roll it up you're going to 8 wing"

I don't do a thing except braid my hair, roll my coveralls down and prepare for battle. 30 minutes later the correctional officers show up and open the cuff port and say "Cuff up Thorson"

I reply "Nope"

They say "Thorson your being released cuff up"

"Nope, I ain't going anywhere"

"Thorson you're being released. Don't you want to get out of IMU?"

"Nope I like it here"

"Well you can't stay we have our orders, so cuff up."

I smile and reply "Bring the extraction squad if you want this cell"

They say "We will take your TV if you don't cuff up"

I walk over to the TV and unplug it and set it down by the door and say "Take it I didn't want it in the first place"

I step back to the back wall and they open the door just long enough to grab the TV. Then they leave.

Everyone is laughing at the correctional officers. They are stuck and don't know how to deal with a situation like this. None of them want to come into my cell either.

About 4 hours later 3 correctional officers come to my door and say "Thorson roll it up your being released. Are you ready?"

"I am not leaving without a fight"

"Ok" They open my door and slide my TV back inside.

Another six months go by and now I am really comfortable so I am telling guys we ought to just refuse to leave IMU and clog it up. Then what is the administration going to do when the Lifers all decide that the single man cell and room service are gravy and refuse to leave the IMU? But so far I don't have any takers. So I am talking to guys that only have like a year left, trying to get them to just finish their time out in IMU. Even that will create a small clog and screw up the IMU Programs. Because if we fill up all the IMU cells what are they going to threaten the rest of the felons with? But no one is up to it so the plan falls by the wayside.

They come and get me for another six month progress hearing and again say they are going to release me. But I still have about 4 months of sanctions left that they won't drop them. So I tell them forget it I ain't going.

They then are fed up with me and ship me off to Clallam Bay Corrections Center IMU. Typical DOC Procedures 'if we can't deal with it pass the buck' give the problem to another prison.

So I get there and Clallam Bay wants to release me after the intake hearing.

So I ask "Will my sanctions follow me from W.S.P.?"

They say "Yes".

So I tell them "I ain't leaving IMU. I am cool with the single man cell and room service".

"Mr. Thorson that kind of behavior won't be tolerated here. You will go to where you are assigned".

"What ya gonna do if I don't, beat me up?"

"No Mr. Thorson you will go where you are assigned and that will be the end of it. Now go get ready to move to where ever you're assigned"

I laugh and say "Ok"

The correctional officers escort me back to my cell and uncuff me. About three hours later two correctional officers show up at my door and say "Thorson roll it up and cuff up"

I reply "Nope I ain't going anywhere"

"Come on Thorson you have to go we have our orders."

"If you want me out of this cell go get the Extraction Squad" (Do you see a pattern of civil disobedience developing here?)

So they left and infracted me for refusing a housing assignment.

At the infraction hearing the Hearing Officer asked me how long I planned on staying in IMU. I told him until November 22 2027 or until I was paroled whichever came first.

I was transferred to McNeil Island IMU after about a year because they couldn't figure out how to get me to move back into the main

Population. Clallam Bay didn't want me there taking up one of their IMU cells and trying to talk other prisoners into not releasing and clogging up their IMU Program.

Well, when I get to McNeil I see ole Chucky Cheese. He is a Rat from Walla Walla who kept coming out of P.C. to population every 6 months or so and he would get beat up then put back into P.C. I haven't seen Ole Chucky Cheese in years. Maybe here at McNeil Island no one knew who he was. But in the joint you can never hide from your past. Someone somewhere will remember you.

So I yell out as he is going to the shower "Hey, Chucky Cheese! Is this where you have been hiding the past few years?"

He spun around mad clear through. He is a big healthy Snitch so can intimidate some felons. He bellows "Who said that?"

I reply "Thor"

He just puts his head down and goes back to his cell. I don't know his story or how he got the snitch jacket put on him. But I do know he will fight to protect his name if he has to. But in my case he knows he can't win and nothing would change if I kicked his ass. But also we will never be on the same yard as long as we are in IMU as this is isolation we all yard alone.

Well about a month after I am in McNeil Island the Parole Board comes to see me.

They ask why I am in IMU. I tell them because I like a single man cell and the room service is great. They inquire as to how long I plan on remaining in IMU. I tell them until I am released from prison.

They reply "Well we are not going to Parole you from IMU."

"So, you're not going to Parole me anyways so why should I care?"

They then say "Mr. Thorson you haven't given us a reason to consider you for Parole."

"What do you want? Tell me the formula to get paroled and I will try to do it."

"There is no formula Mr. Thorson. We will just know when you're ready."

"Fine, so basically you're saying you're never going to parole me anyway so there is no point in my trying to impress you right?"

"Alright Mr. Thorson, if you get out of IMU, we will let you go to any Institution you request and if you give us 2 years infraction free we will grant you Parole."

"Can I get that in writing?"

"It will be stated in our Reason and Decisions and you will get a copy of that Mr. Thorson."

"Ok. Deal"

The thing was they had made deals like this with me before and never kept their word. In other deals they told me if I completed the drug and alcohol program they would release me. I did and I was due to be released in 1993 but then I was 90 days short the Parole Board gave me 5 more years no reason.

In 1995 they told me if I completed the stress and anger management program they would release me. It was a lie.

In 1997 they said if I completed the victims awareness program they would release me. This was another lie and they had dangled the carrot in front of my nose a lot of time before and always snatched it away just as I reached for it.

But what choice do you have? You must reach for it every time like a drowning man reaches for a life line. It is your only hope.

So I tell them I want to go to WSR at Monroe. They say no problem. That was another lie. They sent me to WCC at Shelton.

These people wouldn't know the truth if is snuck up and bit them in the ass.

Well you can only dangle the carrot so many time before even a mule will quit reaching for it. This is the last time I will reach for it. If they are lying they are dying,

Chapter Thirty Five

I arrive in Shelton and am put in Pine Hall. I take my boxes down to my cell and go to see what this place is like. I have never been in the population part of this prison before.

So I get my cup of coffee and go out to the dayroom. I notice a hotshot. So that's cool. All the cells have state provided color TVs.

I meet Dan and he is running the Wiccan Group here and works in the library. He tells me there is an opening in the library and at movement I should go up there and put in an application. So at the next movement he is going to work so we walk up there together. I fill out an application and he kind of shows me the ropes. But man this guy wouldn't know the truth either, he is always telling tall tales about everything from being a Navy SEAL to waiting outside a castle for 3 years in Ireland to learn Wicca.

I then return to the unit at next movement. When I get back there one of the unit Correctional Officers confronts me and asks for my ID card then wants to know where I have been.

He doesn't really care he is just trying to let me know he is the big dog on this yard. So I tell him I went to the library to apply for work. He says "Who told you to?"

"No one I just heard there was an opening and went"

"You can't just go where ever you want whenever you want to. You have to go at movement or get a pass from the control booth"

"I went at last movement. Isn't that when I can go to the library?"

"Don't get cute with me Mr. Thorson. Go lock up."

I head back into my hall way but stop in the dayroom for a cup of hot water for coffee. The guard is on the intercom "Thorson lock up right now"

"I am I just am getting a cup of water for coffee"

"LOCK UP!!" so I do. I no sooner get into my cell and over the intercom I hear "Thorson report to the Sergeants' Office"

So I turn around and walk back to the control booth and wait by the Sergeants' Office door.

The same stupid Correctional Officers opens the door from the inside and I walk in. a little Lady Sergeant is sitting behind a big desk. Sergeant Sanchez.

She says "Do you mind telling me what you think you're doing?"

I reply at a loss "I have no idea what you're talking about"

The Correctional Officers then states "The library just called and said he was up there harassing them about giving him a job"

"That's a lie!"

He says "Sergeant Sanchez you know I don't lie, my integrity is very important to me."

"Well then, quit lying, I told you I was at the library when you asked me where I was. If the library had called you would have already known where I was."

Sergeant Sanchez says "Watch it Mr. Thorson. My officers don't lie"

"Well he just did. Check this out there is a room for me out in IMU and my stuff is still packed."

Sergeant Sanchez says "You don't want to go back to IMU."

"Yes I do"

"Why?"

"So I don't have to put up with idiots like you"

The sergeant lost her composure and yells at me "Thorson go lock up"

So I figure I am going to the hole. No big deal. Fuck the Parole Board and their deal they will come with another one I am betting.

Well in about 20 minutes I am called back to the sergeant's office. Sergeant Sanchez says "Thorson where are you working?"

"No where I just got here and was trying to find work in the library"

"I got you a job working in the Inmate Kitchen. Take this slip of paper and report to the kitchen for work."

"Nope, I ain't working in the kitchen"

"Mr. Thorson you will do as you're told while you are here."

"Look lady I am going to do whatever I want to do and if by chance what I do coincides with your rules fine but if it doesn't I flat don't give a fuck. I am not one of these sissy inmates you're used to pushing around. Check my central file I am a convict, lady."

"Inmate Thorson, Take this pass and report to the kitchen and do it now"

"Yes Ma'am" I take her paper and go back to my cell and throw it in the toilet.

She must have thought she had won. She didn't bother me for about 2 days. Then she sees me in the day room and call's me to the office.

"Mr. Thorson aren't you suppose to be at work?"

"No I haven't found a job yet"

"What happened to the kitchen job?"

"Oh that? I never went."

A Correctional Officer over hearing us takes out his cuffs and says "Well maybe you want to do a little time in the hole"

I reply "You'll never get me out of the hole again"

Sergeant Sanchez says "No he wants to go to the hole he is not to be infracted or sent to the hole for anything unless he attacks a Correctional Officer or inmate." Now she said this right in front of me, I guess to let me know she was in control and wasn't going to let me have my way. But all I took from it was I had free rein to do whatever I wanted to as long as I didn't get physical.

She then tells the Correctional Officer "Give Mr. Thorson another pass to the Inmate Kitchen for work and call the kitchen and tell them to expect him."

I take the pass and say "Well I reckon you can make me go but I won't work there and then they will fire me or toss me in the hole."

Then I start walking to the kitchen. On the yard speakers I hear "Thorson report back to your unit" I ignore it and continue heading to the kitchen. Again "Thorson report back to your unit now." I ignore it. At a guards booth called the point a Correctional Officer confronts me.

"Thorson you're wanted back at your unit"

"So?"

"Didn't you hear them calling for you over the intercom? That means turn around and go back where you came from."

"I have a pass to go to the kitchen for work"

"Thorson I am not letting you through the gate go back to your unit."

"Ok if you say so"

So I get back to the unit and The Custody Unit Supervisor (CUS) is waiting for me, Mr. McGregor.

He takes me into his office and politely says "Sit down Mr. Thorson."

I do and he continues "What seems to be the problem here?"

So I give him my version of what has happened in the last couple days and tell him I am used to having a little more respect shown to me.

He says "You have to show a little respect to get respect."

I tell him "I always give respect to everyone until they prove themselves unworthy of my respect."

So he says "You don't have to work in the kitchen where would you like to work."

"Ground maintenance or the green house"

"I'll see what I can do but until then will you give me your word you will try to keep a low profile?"

"Yep, ya got my word."

So the next day I am walking with Dan back from chow and I am talking about the other two halls dumping sawdust on the flower beds and how that takes the nitrogen out of the soil and makes it hard for the plants to get the nutrients they need. This well dressed woman was walking behind us close enough for her to overhear what was being said. So she asked me "Do you know a lot about landscaping?"

I replied "Yes Ma'am I have a certificate in horticulture." I didn't really pay attention to who she was. I thought she might be a counselor or something.

When we get back to the unit CO Dyer comes to my cell and says the Sergeant Sanchez wants to hire me around the unit first as a tier porter until the mound porter job comes open.

I tell him "Nope don't want the job."

He says "Will you tell me why? I will have to tell her something"

"Sure tell her I can't work for an idiot"

Dyer looks at me then says "I am not repeating that, I'll let you tell her that. But you might want to think it over it is a plush job" then he leaves

Half an hour later I hear over the intercom "Thorson report to the Sergeants' Office." So I go and there is Sergeant Sanchez all dressed up like a woman. It is she who was talking to me on the way back from chow. I didn't recognize her.

She says "Mr. Thorson I think we got off on the wrong foot and I would like to make amends by offering you a job here in the unit. I would like to put you on as mound porter but I won't have an opening for about a month. So I am starting you as tier porter on your tier until the mound porter job comes open. So will you do that?"

"Nope"

"The tier porter position is just temporary I just want to be sure to keep you available when the mound porter position comes open."

"Nope I don't want the job"

Shocked she replied "Why not?"

"Because I won't work for an asshole"

She then angrily says "Well, you have the job! On May 1st about 7000 seedling flowers are going to show up on the mound and if you don't plant them they can just dry up and blow away! Now get the hell out of my office."

So I do start doing the tier porter job. I work 7 days a week even though only 5 days are required. It is just sweeping mopping and cleaning the showers and if I don't do it no one else will clean up after themselves.

So May 1st rolls around and CO Dyer comes and tells me I am now the Mound Porter and the seedlings are on the mound. I tell him "So what" and he leaves.

I walk out there and sure enough there is a sea of color. Well, I could let them die but it is not in my soul to do so.

I go to the Sergeants' Office and knock on the door. Sergeant Sanchez answers the door. I say "Ok, What do you want done with all those flowers?"

She says "I don't give a damn what you do with them!" and slams the door in my face.

I knock on the door again. Sergeant Sanchez opens in and says "What the hell do you want now?"

I reply meekly "Can I have some tools or would you have me dig the holes with my fingers?"

She turns to CO Dyer and says "Get this man whatever he wants then get him out of my office."

So to cause a little hate and malcontent I planted an Indian Medicine Wheel, a Christian Cross, a Pagan Shield knot, a pagan Valknot and then Smile Now Cry Later faces/masks all out of flowers. Then I edged the beds and took the sharp corners off the beds and gave them a smooth flowing roundness to them. I was called into the office and told I was not to enlarge the flower beds anymore. I told them I wasn't enlarging them I was just reshaping them to Dragon Feng Shui. So the energy could flow correctly. The Sergeant who loves dragons bought right in to it.

But shortly I ran out of flowers. So I was walking around and the other two halls had a lot of extra flowers the mound porters didn't want to plant. So I took them. Then again I ran out of flowers so I went looking with my wheelbarrow and found a bunch of unplanted flowers up by the administration building that no one was guarding so I loaded them up. A Correctional Officer took notice and said "Who are you"

I replied "I am the mound porter"

He said "What are you doing up here?"

I replied "I am the mound porter"

He said "Ok"

So I get back to the unit with my ill gotten gains. The sergeant called me to her office. So I figured naturally I would have to give back all those plants.

Sergeant Sanchez asks "Where were you?"

I reply "Why?"

"I just got a call from an officer that said you were in front of the admin building"

"If you knew where I was why did you ask?"

"Who told you that you could go there?"

"No one"

"Did you get a pass or ask permission to go up there?"

"No"

Sergeant Sanchez sternly says "Why Not? That is a secure area"

I said "Because, if I had asked someone might have said no."

She looks at me as if I had lost my mind. Then says "Ok"

She doesn't do anything to me for this little breach of the rules because she really like flowers and plants and she is impressed with the way Pine Hall is looking.

Pine Hall was the worst looking of the three General Population units. But now it is the best looking.

One weekend day I got the shears out and cut all the hedges to look like the hedges in the Super Mario game, they were uninteresting square blobs before I started. When the CUS and Sergeant came to work on Monday morning I was called into the office and the CUS asked "Who did you ask before you reshaped the hedges?"

I replied "No one"

He then said "Why didn't you ask someone before taking on that endeavor?"

Before I could reply Sergeant Sanchez cut in and said "He didn't ask because if he had, someone might have told him no."

The CUS looked at her. She blurted out "I have had this conversation with him before." But she was smiling to see the CUS have a little of the medicine she was forced to swallow on a regular basis, on his suggestion that she just be tolerant with me.

About this time I think she realized I wasn't just being mean to her, it was how I am and she began to like me.

So from this point on I could do no wrong in her eyes and she gave me free rein to run amuck. She would bring in plants I asked for if she had to go buy them with her own money. She never broke the rules nor let me flagrantly break a rule or disrespect a Correctional Officer. But she let me bend rules and gave me the benefit of the doubt. So in truth I came to love this bull headed little sergeant.

So after two years it came time to see the Parole Board again.

I had to go see the shrink and get evaluated and after running all the tests the shrink asks me did I ever get any feedback on tests like this before?

I reply "No why?"

He says, "I have never seen tests like these before from anyone in prison. Your IQ is in the top 3% of the United States. What are you still doing here?"

I told him "Oh I could get out but I am trying to do it legally this time."

He is amazed and it shows in his voice when he says "You can't really get out of here."

So I say "Wanna take a walk with me?" he doesn't so I just explain to him two ways I could leave today.

Then he tells me that the finding of someone with an IQ in my range and in a situation like mine, was that I have a 70% chance of being a psychopath and that my climb from the bottom of the pecking order to the top in such a short time seems to favor this diagnosis. So he has me do another whole battery of tests and when he is done he prepares his report for The Parole Board. He tells me this is the longest report he has ever done on a prisoner.

Now after I read it, I am thinking it is not a very flattering report. But what can I do? Beating up the shrink won't help my case much. So I tell Sergeant Sanchez and she goes and reads the report. Then she tells me she will go to The Parole Board hearing with me and put in a good word. But I am thinking, this is The Parole Boards last chance anyway. They always give a deferred decision so they aren't in the room when the felon gets the bad news if it is bad news. So I am going to be good this time as I have done just about everything a felon can do, taken the drug & alcohol program, victims' awareness program and all the other self help programs available.

So if I get bad news after this hearing ... the next hearing will go my way. I will go in there with my shank and jump the table and just start stabbing the shit out of whoever is there. They don't search you before you go in the room and there are no metal detectors to pass through. So after this I won't have to be good or wonder if I am ever getting out, I will know getting out from then on, will not be in the realm of possibilities and I won't have to listen to them give me fault hope and promises they never keep.

You can only tease a dangerous animal so many times before he gets fed up and teaches you why they call him dangerous.

So the day comes, Sergeant Sanchez, CUS McGregor and I go into the Parole hearing.

The Parole Board looks over my file and then say "Well Mr. Thorson do you have anything to say?"

I Reply "No I don't have anything to say but I have done everything you have asked of me and I believe my Unit Sergeant, Sergeant Sanchez would like to make a few comments on my behalf."

The Board Member says "We don't need to hear from your Sergeant I believe you may have befriended her and her comments would have no bearing on our decision."

The Sergeant turned beet red and she is a strong headed woman and likes to have her say. But she did real good not blowing up and telling the board to kiss her ass as I am sure she wanted to.

So the CUS who didn't need the boards ok to talk, pretty much told them in his words what the sergeant wanted to tell them as he too knew the little sergeant was a powder keg when things didn't go her way.

Then the board said they would let me know by mail in the next 30 days what their decision was and we all left.

When we got outside the sergeant blew her cool and ranted and raved all the way back to the unit. She told me not to get my hopes up as she didn't think they were going to release me.

Well the 30 days went past and the mail came from Olympia. They paroled me to my last escape. But put the stipulation in that if I got any Major infractions while doing the 38 months for the last escape they would violate my parole and extent my sentence to the Maximum of 11/23/2027. Again they did not certify or give me any good time as was their usual procedure in dealing with me.

Well I spread the good news to my fellow felons joyfully and my Sergeant was happy and sad as we had become fast friends. Only 4 guards had I ever made friends with in my 27 years and 2 months, Ms. McGee, Mr. Best, Mr. Edgar and Sergeant Sanchez. There were a lot of other guards I respected, most from the old days when Gladiator School was in all its Deadly Glory. But even though these guards were my friends I never forgot they were guards and never told them anything I didn't want them to know.

Well when the word got out that I couldn't get a major infraction for the next 3 years, a few Correctional Officers and the Chaplain, Gordo swore they would see to it that I wouldn't make it. Dumb move on their part, because if they succeeded in ruining my chance to get out I would have killed them, so they would not have been around to gloat.

But more importantly what I didn't consider, being King for so long the thought that one of my felon enemies would think he had a chance to even some old score never crossed my mind. What I would do to them if they ruined my chance never crossed their mind. But it should have because I would also have killed these idiots for ruining my chances. But they came out of the wood work like roaches in a southern White Castle kitchen after dark.

Up to the plate stepped friends I didn't know I could count on, Fellow Prisoners who stood between me and the other felons so that the next 3 years passed pretty uneventful and I paroled out on November 3rd 2003.

I still had to put up with 5 years of parole under an asshole parole officer who treated me worse than a sex offender and did everything in his power to send me back including making up bullshit. But I survived him too and am now a free man and can tell this story of injustice and corruption in America.

Each time a man stands up for an ideal, or acts to improve the lot of others, or strikes out against injustice, he sends forth a chris ripple of hope...building a current that can sweep down the mightiest walls of oppression and resistance.

Robert F. Kennedy

The shepherd drives the wolf from the sheep's flock for which the sheep thanks the shepherd as his liberator, while the wolf denounces him for the same act as the destroyer of liberty. Plainly, the sheep and the wolf are not agreed upon a definition of liberty.

Abraham Lincoln

If you want to see the scum of society go to a prison parking lot at shift change

Winston Churchill

Your liberty is at risk right now, I know I lost mine in a twinkling. Fight for it or lose it.

Robert Thorson

The End

Would you like to see your manuscript become a book?

If you are interested in becoming a PublishAmerica author, please submit your manuscript for possible publication to us at:

acquisitions@publishamerica.com

You may also mail in your manuscript to:

**PublishAmerica
PO Box 151
Frederick, MD 21705**

www.publishamerica.com

CPSIA information can be obtained at www.ICGtesting.com
Printed in the USA
BVOW010103140911

271188BV00002B/22/P